the Easy Vegetarian Kitchen

50 Classic Recipes with Seasonal Variations
for Hundreds of Fast, Delicious Plant-Based Meals

Erin Alderson

First published in the USA in 2015 by
Fair Winds Press, a member of
Quarto Publishing Group USA Inc.
100 Cummings Center
Suite 406-L
Beverly, MA 01915-6101
www.fairwindspress.com

19 18 17 16 15   1 2 3 4 5

ISBN: 978-1-59233-658-6   *5660   3508   05/15*

Digital edition published in 2015
eISBN: 978-1-62788-284-2

Library of Congress Cataloging-in-Publication Data available

Book and cover design by Kathie Alexander
Page layout by *tabula rasa* graphic design
Photography by Erin Alderson

Printed and bound in China

The information in this book is for educational purposes only.
It is not intended to replace the advice of a physician or
medical practitioner. Please see your health care provider
before beginning any new health program.

To my parents for always encouraging me to try something new.

Contents

Introduction

A few years ago, on a cold January day in snow-covered Illinois, I began dreaming about fresh produce. I'd had enough of winter, and longed for spring—and with it, the return of the farmers' market. I had grand plans for highlighting seasonal produce on my website, naturallyella.com, and with those grand plans came research into local produce. I had frequented the farmers' market every summer, chatting with the farmers and learning plenty, but I still felt like I was missing out on something. At the time, my husband and I were moving around so much that I couldn't have a garden of my own, but I knew I wanted to learn more about how—and where—my food was being grown.

Finally, I stumbled upon a local Community Supported Agriculture (CSA) program. It was a "u-pick" farm, which meant that each week I headed out to the farm to connect with the food that eventually made its way onto my plate. I made the trip every single week, rain or shine, because I enjoyed that connection so much. Being able to pick my own produce and understand its growth cycles was, and still is, an incredibly rewarding experience.

Of course, joining a CSA meant a regular supply of fruits and vegetables, and I realized right away that I needed to change my approach to cooking. Until then, I'd just research recipes that piqued my interest, and base a week of meals around those recipes. But after I became part of a CSA, I stopped basing my meal plans around single recipes, and shifted my focus to working with the produce I picked that week at the farm. To be honest, I wasn't terribly creative at first, but after a little time and practice, challenging myself to come up with new recipes and meals became fun and exciting. I began digging into unusual flavor combinations, learning how to bring out the best in each type of produce.

This philosophy has completely reshaped the way I cook. Today, I pay far less attention to individual recipes; instead, I adapt basic staple recipes to suit the fresh ingredients I have on hand. (I use the term *recipes* lightly because, for a few years, a lot of the recipes in this book weren't even written down! I simply relied on basic measurements that I knew by heart and could tweak as necessary.) And what's more, my husband and I found that our attitudes toward food also changed as a result of this transition. You know those weekday nights when you're convinced there's nothing in the house for dinner? Well, for us, they became a thing of the past, because I'd become a dab hand at making a satisfying meal by tossing together just a few simple, fresh ingredients—no recipe needed. I felt so liberated, because it meant we were much less dependent on processed foods and eating out.

Living in the rural Midwest taught me a lot about the cycle of growing food. From an early age, I knew that rhubarb was a springtime treat, while tomatoes were only really good during the months of July, August, and September. And now that I live in California, I rarely eat much out-of-season produce at all—the fresh taste of in-season fruits and vegetables is just too good. That's why this book provides seasonal adaptations of staple recipes—although the truth is, these meals could easily be made at any time of year.

What Is "Easy Vegetarian"?

So where does the "easy" in the title *The Easy Vegetarian Kitchen* come in? I'll be honest with you: when I first started cooking, I laughed at anyone who said any aspect of it was "easy." For me, of course, *everything* was hard: I was learning. I had more fails in the kitchen than I care to count, but I stuck with it, and began to master the basics. Ultimately, "easy" is a relative term, and what's simple for one person may be more challenging for another. Keeping that in mind, I've done my best to strike a balance between creativity, simplicity, and taste in the recipes in this book.

You'll also find that these recipes are easy to adapt. Each base recipe is followed by four seasonal variations that are inspired by the produce (and the flavors) at that time of year. And that means you get four for the price of one, so to speak. Once you feel confident with one recipe, it's simple to make four other delicious versions of it. And you'll be able to come up with your own takes on the base recipes, depending on the ingredients you have on hand. Got only two of the three produce items a recipe calls for? (I've been there!) No problem. You'll be able to adapt the base recipes to fit whatever's in your fridge.

Finally, please don't assume that every single ingredient needs to be homemade. I try to make things from scratch whenever I can, but the truth is, with long workdays and busy schedules, that's not always possible. So I cheat a little, and you can, too. For instance, if my husband and I are craving pizza after an exhausting day, I'll use premade dough from a supermarket or our local pizza place. I've also been known to pick up store-bought pumpkin purée or corn tortillas in a pinch. After all, we're only human!

Also, the recipes in this book are very indicative of my personal style. They're easy vegetarian recipes that sometimes are also naturally vegan and/or gluten-free. Many of them can be whipped up at a moment's notice, and—even better—you'll be able to reduce your food waste because you'll always have ways to use those bits and pieces that might've lingered in the back of the fridge for an extra day. My hope is that this book will provide you with a reference of delicious, reliable recipes you can make throughout the seasons.

Transitioning to Health

Being vegetarian hasn't always been a way of life for me. In fact, for a good chunk of my life, the words *whole foods* and *unprocessed* weren't even part of my vocabulary. I grew up in a typical middle-class family. We were always on the go, and that meant we ate plenty of prepackaged and fast food, because it was quick and easy. And my eating habits didn't change until my family and I got a serious wake-up call.

I was in my early twenties, and my father and I were playing in an ice hockey game. As he headed to the bench, I noticed that he was short of breath. Turns out he wasn't just fatigued: that shortness of breath turned into a heart attack, which led to a quadruple bypass. My dad's illness was an eye-opening experience for all of us because unless we made some significant changes (and fast), our unhealthy eating habits were going to lead to health problems for the entire family.

From that point forward, I began to weed out the overly processed foods I'd relied on for so long, and started creating well-balanced meals. Over time, I also—slowly—became vegetarian. It was a natural, organic transition: I loved focusing on whole grains, legumes, nuts, and seeds, balanced with a healthy portion of fruits and vegetables. It wasn't easy at first, and for a while I missed my old fast-food favorites, but as time passed, I actually found myself craving the wholesome meals I was already making.

And the final step in my transition to being vegetarian came when I joined a CSA, as my cooking became more and more about showcasing fresh, seasonal produce. That's what really inspired the recipes in this book, as well as the ones on my website. Both of them share a goal: to introduce you and your family to the possibilities of vegetarian meals, whether you want to dive straight into becoming vegetarian or whether you're just looking for a few plant-based meals to add to your weekly routine.

Being an easy vegetarian is simply about eating consistently in a plant-based way for good health. And it's about more than just eating healthfully—it's my hope that these recipes, in their focus on seasonal produce, will help you feel more connected to the food that's on your plate.

1

Stocking the Pantry

After I joined a CSA, I started to experiment with various pantry items, such as grains, legumes, nuts, and seeds. And it was one of the best things I ever did. Keeping a few varieties of grains and legumes around ensures that you'll always have a meal at the ready. Some of these staples do require a bit of prep—certain varieties of beans and grains need to be soaked before cooking, for example—but plenty of others (such as lentils) can be cooked up quickly and easily, and can help bring a meal together in no time flat.

In the following pages, I'll take you through the items I keep stocked in my kitchen. But don't feel you need to rush out and buy everything on my list. Instead, find the items you and your family like, and use them as the building blocks for your own meals. I usually keep a few different grains and two or three types of legumes on hand, and I'll often cook a couple batches of each on the weekend to use in meals during the week.

< Cinnamon Apples with Sorghum-Spelt Granola

Grains

Grains, both with and without gluten, form the backbone of my cooking, either through the whole grain or its flour. I keep around five or six grains in my kitchen, and pick up others from time to time. (Different varieties of grains have different cooking times; a guide to these cooking times can be found on page 186.) And I'll often substitute one grain for another. Quinoa, for instance, makes a lovely sub for brown rice, while spelt or rye flakes are great stand-ins for oats. It's fine to keep small containers of uncooked grains on the counter for quick, everyday use, but for extended storage, it's best to keep grains and flours in airtight containers in the freezer.

Once you know your grains, it's much easier to make meals gluten-free. Oat groats make a nice replacement for wheatberries, while millet, quinoa, and sorghum are my favorite hearty, go-to gluten-free grains when it comes to salads, pilafs, and grain-based side dishes.

Five main grains:

- **Wheat berries:** mainly used to grind flour, but also for salads and breakfast porridge
- **Oats (groats and rolled oats):** for flour, oatmeal, and additions to baked goods
- **Brown rice:** a versatile, go-to grain for main dishes
- **Quinoa:** secondary go-to grain, great for main dishes, salads, and soups
- **Farro:** primarily to keep on hand for the risotto on page 140, but also for grinding into flour

Other grains to work into your meals:

- Millet
- Amaranth
- Einkorn
- Sorghum
- Kamut (whole and rolled flakes)
- Spelt (whole and rolled flakes)
- Rye (whole and rolled flakes)
- Polenta
- Barley (whole and rolled flakes)

Legumes

Even though I love vegetarian recipes, I've never been overly excited about processed vegetarian protein, such as tofu or seitan, and have always preferred legumes, such as chickpeas, black beans, and lentils. You don't have to look much further to find a foundation for a hearty and filling meal. Legumes take center stage in the black bean tacos on page 122 or the lentil stew on page 76. In fact, these three legumes show up more often than not in my main meals, and they're easy to keep on hand. In terms of prep, black beans and chickpeas require an extended soaking time before cooking, but lentils need no soaking at all, and cook up in roughly 20 minutes. Beans should be stored in an airtight container in a cool, dry place.

Three main legumes:

- **Chickpeas:** used for just about everything. I grind them into flour in their dried form, and when they're cooked, I use them on salads, in curries, and puréed as hummus.
- **Black beans:** the main filling for my tacos and enchiladas (page 146). They can also be ground into flour.
- **Lentils:** a base for quick meals and salads. Keep a couple of different varieties on hand, such as red and black, because their textures are different once they're cooked.

Other legumes to experiment with:

- White beans
- Black-eyed peas
- Split peas
- Kidney beans

Nuts and Seeds

Nuts and seeds serve a twofold purpose: they provide a little extra protein, and add texture and flavor to a dish. I love topping salads with a few extra nuts and seeds, or sprinkling them over a finished dish for extra crunch—and I've also been known to sprinkle a handful of toasted sesame seeds on a soba noodle bowl or potstickers (page 80) for a final hit of flavor.

Nuts are best kept fresh and should be stored in the refrigerator or freezer. Because nuts can become rancid and it's not always easy to tell how fresh they are upon purchase, I usually keep a small stash of nuts in my refrigerator and replace as needed.

Nuts and seeds I keep on hand:

- Almonds
- Pecans
- Walnuts
- Hazelnuts
- Pistachios
- Sesame seeds
- Sunflower seeds
- Pumpkin seeds

Herbs and Spices

I know I've tucked my herbs and spices checklist into the middle of this chapter, but don't be fooled! Herbs and spices are your not-so-secret weapons when it comes to great vegetarian cooking. They're what take a dish from "just okay" to absolutely phenomenal. That's why I always keep my spice cabinet well stocked, and rely on my small, herb-filled patio garden for fresh herbs. Some co-ops and natural food stores sell herbs and spices in bulk, which makes it easy to buy small amounts, keeping their flavors as fresh as possible.

Herbs to have on hand (primarily fresh, but occasionally dried):

- Thyme
- Dill
- Mint
- Basil
- Parsley
- Sage
- Oregano
- Cilantro
- Rosemary

Spices you'll find on my spice rack:

- Smoked paprika
- Cinnamon
- Chili powder
- Nutmeg (whole)
- Cumin (seeds and ground)
- Cloves
- Ginger
- Coriander (seeds and ground)
- Fenugreek
- Turmeric
- Cardamom

Dairy

I grew up during the low-fat phase of American food culture. Everything—even cookies—was being marketed as low-fat. It took me a while to shake the aftereffects of the low-fat craze, but I've finally succeeded. Now, I'm a champion of whole milk, heavy cream, and butter. That said, moderation is key: I always try to reach a healthy balance of fats and fresh foods, such as fruits, vegetables, grains, and legumes. Feel free to substitute lower-fat milk in recipes that call for the full-fat variety, but be aware that some of the recipes rely on the extra fats the whole milk provides.

Dairy items to keep in your fridge:

- Whole milk
- Heavy cream
- Plain, whole-milk Greek-style yogurt
- Hard cheeses (an assortment—many of them feature in these recipes)
- Eggs

Fats and Sweeteners

My take on fats and sweeteners is just like my attitude to dairy foods: I use them wisely. I always choose good-quality fats and, for the most part, I try to stay away from refined sugars (although there is the occasional use for confectioners' sugar or cane sugar). Go ahead and substitute liberally here: I like to use coconut oil or walnut oil in place of butter in sweet recipes, for instance, or I'll replace honey with maple syrup or brown rice syrup, which is great for making a meal vegan.

Fats/Oils

- Olive oil
- Butter
- Coconut oil
- Walnut or almond oil
- Peanut oil
- Sesame oil

Sweeteners

- Maple syrup
- Honey
- Sorghum syrup
- Molasses
- Muscovado sugar
- Brown rice syrup

Everything Else

The above lists cover about 95 percent of what you'll find in my cupboards—but here are a few extra items that help me round out meals:

- Soy or tamari sauce
- Hot sauce
- Vinegars (balsamic, champagne, apple cider)
- Condiments (mustard, mayonnaise)

Again, these aren't hard-and-fast rules. Experiment with your favorite combinations, and don't be afraid to substitute according to what you happen to have on hand. Many of the recipes in this book can easily be made gluten-free or vegan. If you're wondering how to replace dairy products with vegan-friendly alternatives, try using almond milk in place of whole milk, and replace cheese with your favorite vegan cheese substitute.

2

Breakfast

I've been a morning person for about as long as I can remember. Even as a teenager, I'd wake up early to have coffee with my aunt and uncle while my cousins slept away their entire summer vacations. I took special pride in never sleeping past 10 a.m. (although I'm not sure exactly *why* I was so proud of that), and I never had a love-hate relationship with my alarm clock: I always jumped straight out of bed. Although some of these habits have changed as I've gotten older, mornings are still my favorite part of the day. I love those first few sips of fresh, hot coffee; the cool, refreshing air on my morning walks; and breakfast. Oh, I love breakfast.

My romance with breakfast has developed over time. When I was younger, I, like lots of people, never took the time to prepare and eat breakfast, and—at best—would grab a granola bar while running out the door to work. But I realized how much I missed my morning breakfast routine when I worked in a bakery. Early mornings were the order of the day, and by the time my usual breakfast hour rolled around, I'd already been at work for three hours and had eaten my fair share of pastries. The quiet time and good food I had once taken for granted was now gone—and I really missed it.

These days, breakfast is a far cry from the mornings of hastily eaten granola bars. I usually alternate between eggs, yogurt, and oatmeal, depending on what sounds good and what kind of produce I have on hand. This collection of breakfast recipes runs the gamut from quick morning breakfasts, such as oatmeal and omelets, to recipes that are perfect for a lazy weekend brunch, such as quiches and Dutch babies. Of course, you don't have to reserve these recipes for mornings only—breakfast can be nourishing any time of day. (My husband and I eat breakfast for dinner at least once a week!)

< Maple Apple Oats

Oatmeal

Oatmeal made from rolled oats is one of the most overlooked breakfast items. When I was growing up, I'd watch my father eat sugar-laden instant oatmeal topped with dried fruit, which I thought was completely normal. Turns out that quick, prepackaged oats are extremely overrated. The processing strips out many nutrients, replacing them with sugar, preservatives, and artificial flavorings. Old-fashioned oats are an inexpensive whole grain that cook up quickly, and work as a lovely neutral palette for seasonal produce.

There are a few different varieties of oats, all of which have a place in my vegetarian kitchen. Rolled oats (also known as old-fashioned oats) are made by steaming and flattening a whole oat groat, and I use them most often. Instant and quick oats are slightly thinner than rolled oats, and the end result is mushier. Steel-cut oats, also referred to as Irish oats, get their name from the metal blade that cuts a groat into smaller pieces; groats that are ground into small pieces with a stone form Scottish oats. All these varieties are still considered whole grain, because even though processing grinds or flattens oat groats, all the nutrients are still intact! Give each variety a try, and find your favorite.

When cooking oats, I'm fairly free with the amount of liquid I use. If it looks like the oats are absorbing liquid before they are tender, or if I want more of a porridge-like consistency, I add a bit of extra liquid to the mix. Keep an eye on the oats while cooking, and adjust the consistency as you like. To coax even more flavor from your oats, try toasting them in 1 tablespoon (14 g) of butter for 4 to 5 minutes until the oats are lightly browned and smell slightly nutty. Then, cook as usual.

Morning Oats

YIELD: 2 REGULAR SERVINGS OR 1 HUNGRY SERVING

1 cup (100 g) rolled oats
1 cup (240 ml) whole milk
1 cup (240 ml) water
1 tablespoon (15 ml) maple syrup
½ teaspoon vanilla extract
⅛ teaspoon sea salt

Combine all the ingredients in a medium saucepan. Bring to a boil, reduce to a simmer, and cook until the oats are tender and have thickened, 12 to 15 minutes. Divide between 2 bowls and top with your favorite fruit, nuts, and/or a splash of cream.

 Oat Cook Times for 2 Servings:

1 cup (100 g) rolled oats
2 cups (480 ml) liquid
Simmer for 12 to 15 minutes

1 cup (100 g) steel-cut oats
3½ cups (840 ml) liquid
Simmer for 22 to 25 minutes

1 cup (100 g) Scottish oats
3 cups (720 ml) liquid
Simmer for 22 to 25 minutes

SPRING

Roasted Strawberry and Pistachio

YIELD: 2 SERVINGS

· ·

1 recipe Morning Oats (page 14)
2 cups (340 g) sliced strawberries
1½ teaspoons maple syrup, divided
¼ cup (35 g) pistachio pieces

Preheat the oven to 400°F (200°C, or gas mark 6). Toss the strawberries with 1 teaspoon of the maple syrup and place in a single layer in a roasting pan. Toss the pistachios with the remaining ½ teaspoon maple syrup and spread on a baking tray. Bake the pistachios for 10 minutes and the strawberries for 15 minutes. Top the oatmeal with the strawberries and a sprinkle of pistachios.

 SUMMER

Mixed-Berry Overnight Oats

YIELD: 2 SERVINGS

· ·

1 cup (240 ml) whole milk
1 cup (100 g) rolled oats
¼ cup (25 g) sliced almonds
1 cup (145 g) mixed berries: blueberries, blackberries, raspberries
½ teaspoon vanilla extract
2 teaspoons honey

The night before, combine all the ingredients in a bowl. Cover and refrigerate overnight. Serve cold the next morning.

FALL

Maple Apple

YIELD: 2 SERVINGS

• •

1 recipe Morning Oats (page 14)
1 medium apple, peeled and cut into ¼-inch (6 mm) cubes
  (about 1½ cups, or 180 g)
1 tablespoon (15 ml) maple syrup
¼ teaspoon cinnamon
¼ teaspoon freshly grated ginger
2 tablespoons (30 ml) heavy cream
2 tablespoons (14 g) pecan pieces, for serving

Prepare oats as directed but omit the maple syrup in the base recipe. While the oats cook, add the cubed apple, maple syrup, cinnamon, and ginger to a saucepan over medium-low heat and cook until the apples are tender, 6 to 7 minutes. Remove from the heat and stir in the heavy cream. Let sit until the oats are done, 5 to 6 minutes. Top the oats with the apple mixture and a sprinkle of pecans.

 WINTER

Roasted Sweet Potato and Fried Egg

YIELD: 2 SERVINGS

• •

1 recipe Morning Oats (page 14)
2 cups (220 g) sweet potato, peeled and cut into ¼-inch
  (6 mm) cubes
1 tablespoon (15 ml) olive oil, divided
½ teaspoon black pepper
¼ teaspoon sea salt
2 large eggs
1 ounce (28 g) shredded fontina cheese

Preheat the oven to 400°F (200°C, or gas mark 6). Toss the sweet potatoes, 1½ teaspoons (7.5 ml) of the olive oil, pepper, and salt together in a roasting pan and spread the potatoes in a single layer. Roast until the potatoes are tender, 20 to 25 minutes.

While the oats cook, heat the remaining 1½ teaspoons (7.5 ml) oil in a large skillet over medium-low heat. Carefully crack the eggs into the skillet and cook until the whites are set, 2 to 3 minutes. Flip and continue to cook the eggs until the yolks are as firm as you like them, 2 minutes for over-easy or 4 minutes for over-hard. When the oatmeal is done, stir in the cheese until melted. Divide the oats between 2 bowls and top each with half the sweet potatoes and a fried egg.

 Roasted squash, such as butternut, works well in place of sweet potatoes.

Frittata

Eggs turn up in just about every one of my meals, and often serve as a bridge between my husband's meals and my own. He isn't vegetarian, and he knows he feels better when he eats plenty of protein. That means weekday breakfasts revolve around eggs, in one form or another. I might whip up a fried egg and cheese sandwich for my husband so that he can grab-and-go, while my breakfast is (thankfully!) more relaxed, and usually involves either the omelet recipe on page 30 or this frittata.

I like to think of frittatas as a kind of simple, crustless quiche. They come together quickly, and can be used as a blank slate for just about any type of produce, accompanied by a sprinkle of fresh herbs and a smattering of cheese. Traditional Italian frittatas often incorporate pasta, but I skip the pasta in favor of leftover whole grains, such as quinoa, millet, or barley. This frittata is the perfect way to use up any leftovers from the previous night's dinner.

Leftover frittata can also be saved and eaten over the next few days. Occasionally, I'll eat it at room temperature, but you can reheat the frittata by covering and cooking it at 400°F (200°C, or gas mark 6) for 8 to 10 minutes until warm. I've also been known to eat a wedge of frittata with a side salad for a quick and healthy lunch.

Basic Frittata

YIELD: 4 SERVINGS

• •

1½ teaspoons (7.5 ml) olive oil
8 large or extra-large eggs
½ cup (120 ml) whole milk
½ teaspoon sea salt
½ teaspoon black pepper
2 ounces (56 g) shredded cheese

Preheat the oven to 425°F (220°C, or gas mark 7). Heat the olive oil in an 8-inch (20 cm) cast-iron or other oven-safe skillet over medium-low heat.

In a large bowl, whisk together the eggs, milk, salt, and pepper. Pour into the skillet and cook for 5 to 6 minutes, until the bottom is set. Sprinkle the cheese on top. Transfer to the oven and bake for another 12 to 16 minutes, until the frittata has puffed up, doesn't jiggle, and is beginning to brown. Remove and let cool slightly before slicing. Store leftover frittata in the refrigerator.

SPRING

Asparagus and Goat Cheese

YIELD: 4 SERVINGS

. . . .

1 recipe Basic Frittata (page 17)
1 tablespoon (15 ml) olive oil, divided
¼ cup (25 g) sliced green garlic
8 ounces (225 g) asparagus, diced
¼ teaspoon red pepper flakes
3 ounces (84 g) soft goat cheese

In a cast-iron skillet, heat the olive oil over medium-low heat and add the green garlic. Cook until tender and fragrant, 3 to 4 minutes. Stir in the diced asparagus and red pepper flakes. Continue cooking until the asparagus is bright green and slightly tender, 4 to 5 minutes.

Continue with the instructions for the frittata, pouring the egg mixture over the cooked asparagus and omitting the cheese from the base recipe. Sprinkle the goat cheese on top before placing the frittata in the oven.

 SUMMER

Sweet Corn and Red Pepper

YIELD: 4 SERVINGS

. . . .

1 recipe Basic Frittata (page 17)
1 tablespoon (15 ml) olive oil
¼ red onion, minced
½ red pepper, seeded and minced
1 cup (140 g) sweet corn kernels (1 large ear)
2 tablespoons (3 g) minced cilantro
3 ounces (85 g) crumbled cotija cheese
1 ripe avocado, sliced into wedges, for serving
1 lime, sliced into wedges, for serving

In a cast-iron skillet, heat the olive oil over low heat. Add the onion and red pepper, cooking until the onion is soft and fragrant, 4 to 5 minutes. Stir in the corn and continue to cook for another 6 to 7 minutes. Transfer the mixture to a bowl and mix in the cilantro.

Continue with the instructions for frittata, pouring the egg mixture into the skillet and omitting the cheese from the base recipe. Before placing the frittata in the oven, evenly distribute the corn mixture over the eggs and sprinkle with the crumbled cotija cheese. Serve the frittata with the wedges of avocado and lime.

Garlicky Spinach and Quinoa Frittata >

FALL

Garlicky Spinach and Quinoa

YIELD: 4 SERVINGS

. . . .

1 recipe Basic Frittata (page 17)
1 tablespoon (15 ml) olive oil
1 clove garlic, minced
2 cups (80 g) packed, shredded spinach
½ cup (70 g) cooked quinoa
3 ounces (84 g) shredded mozzarella

Heat the olive oil in a cast-iron skillet over low heat. Add the garlic and cook for 1 minute, until fragrant. Turn off the heat, add the spinach, and cover the skillet. Let sit until the spinach is slightly wilted, 3 to 4 minutes. Transfer to a bowl, add the quinoa, stir to combine, and set aside.

Continue with the instructions for the frittata, pouring the egg mixture into the skillet and omitting the cheese in the base recipe. Before placing the frittata in the oven, sprinkle the spinach mixture and cheese over the eggs.

 WINTER

Curried Butternut Squash and Havarti

YIELD: 4 SERVINGS

. . . .

1 recipe Basic Frittata (page 17)
2 cups (200 g) cubed butternut squash
⅓ white onion, sliced
¼ cup (46 g) plain yogurt
2 tablespoons (12 g) curry powder
½ cup (76 g) cooked millet
2 ounces (56 g) shredded Havarti cheese

Preheat the oven to 400°F (200°C, or gas mark 6). In a roasting pan, combine the butternut squash, onion, yogurt, and curry powder. Cook for 20 to 25 minutes, until the squash is tender when pierced with a knife. Toss the roasted squash with the cooked millet.

Continue with the instructions for the frittata, pouring the egg mixture into the skillet and omitting the cheese in the base recipe. Before placing the frittata in the oven, sprinkle the butternut squash mixture and shredded Havarti over the eggs.

Muffins

When I was in college, I always did my best to schedule classes in the afternoon—not so I could sleep, but so I could get all my homework done. For most of my life, I've known that my productivity levels head straight downhill after lunch, so if I wanted to get anything done, it had to happen in the morning. Part of my homework routine included a trip to the local coffee shop, where I'd hunker down with a big cup of coffee and a muffin. These days, I tend to reach for healthier snacks, but I still keep a small stash of muffins around for those mornings when I need a little something extra.

Over the years I've transformed my muffins. Instead of using white flour and processed sugar, I incorporate whole wheat flour and natural sugars, such as maple syrup and honey, as often as possible. The texture is slightly different, but I love the complexity the natural ingredients bring to the muffins. Try using whole wheat pastry flour, which can be found in natural food stores (and the occasional supermarket). If that's unavailable, unbleached all-purpose flour will work just as well.

Also, I like to freeze a batch of muffins, then thaw them at room temperature as needed. That way, I always have fresh muffins at the ready. And the base recipe is a great template for all sorts of variations, such as fresh berries—or, on occasion, chocolate chips.

Anytime Wheat Muffins

YIELD: 12 MUFFINS

- -

2½ cups (300 g) whole wheat pastry flour
2 teaspoons baking powder
½ teaspoon sea salt
2 large eggs
¾ cup (180 ml) whole milk
½ cup (120 ml) sweetener, such as maple or brown rice syrup
½ cup (112 g) melted butter, cooled
½ teaspoon vanilla extract

Preheat the oven to 375°F (190°C, or gas mark 5) and line a 12-cup muffin pan with liners. In a large bowl, stir together the flour, baking powder, and salt. In a separate bowl, whisk together the eggs, milk, maple syrup, melted butter, and vanilla extract. Pour the wet ingredients into the dry, and mix until just combined. Divide the batter evenly among the 12 muffin cups. Bake for 16 to 18 minutes, until the muffins have domed and spring back when pressed lightly. Transfer the muffins to a rack to cool. Store leftover muffins in an airtight container for 3 to 4 days at room temperature, or freeze for extended storage.

SPRING

Spinach-Ricotta

YIELD: 12 MUFFINS

. . . .

1 recipe Anytime Wheat Muffins (page 21)
1 cup (240 g) whole milk ricotta
1 cup (40 g) packed shredded spinach
3 tablespoons (10 g) diced chives

Prepare the muffins as directed, decreasing the milk to ½ cup (120 ml) and adding the ricotta cheese to the wet ingredients. Fold in the spinach and chives before dividing the batter among the muffin cups.

 SUMMER

Pecan-Peach

YIELD: 12 MUFFINS

. . . .

1 recipe Anytime Wheat Muffins (page 21)
1 teaspoon cinnamon
2 peaches, peeled and cut into ¼-inch (6 mm) cubes
  (about 1½ cups, or 280 g)
½ cup (50 g) pecan meal

Prepare the muffins as directed, adding the cinnamon to the dry ingredients. Fold in the peaches and pecan meal before dividing the batter among the muffin cups.

 For extra peach flavor, try roasting the peaches at 400°F (200°C, or gas mark 6) for 15 minutes before adding them to the muffins.

 FALL

Apple-Oat

YIELD: 12 MUFFINS

. . . .

1 recipe Anytime Wheat Muffins (page 21)
2 teaspoons cinnamon
¼ teaspoon nutmeg
½ teaspoon ginger
¼ teaspoon cloves
1½ cups (225 g) peeled and cubed apple
¼ to ½ cup (25 to 50 g) rolled oats, for topping

Prepare the muffins as directed, adding the cinnamon, nutmeg, ginger, and cloves to the dry ingredients. Fold in the cubed apples before dividing the batter among the muffin cups. Sprinkle the muffins with the oats before baking.

 WINTER

Orange-Poppy Seed

YIELD: 12 MUFFINS

. . . .

1 recipe Anytime Wheat Muffins (page 21)
½ cup (110 g) orange pieces (roughly 1 medium-size orange)
Zest from 1 orange
2 tablespoons (18 g) poppy seeds

Glaze
3 tablespoons (45 ml) orange juice
1 tablespoon (20 g) honey

Prepare the muffins as directed, using orange juice in place of ½ cup (120 ml) of the milk and adding the orange zest and poppy seeds to the dry ingredients before dividing the batter among the muffin cups.

To make the glaze: While the muffins bake, whisk together the orange juice and honey in a small bowl. Allow the muffins to cool for 5 minutes, then dunk the top of the muffin into the glaze. Transfer to a rack to finish cooling.

< Apple-Oat Wheat Muffins

Breakfast Parfait

Even after I learned to cook and bake, I avoided making my own granola. In fact, I never even looked up a recipe for it. Somehow, I'd convinced myself that granola was one of those things that wasn't worth making yourself, and was far easier to buy ready-made. Eventually, I got a job in a bakery, and guess which task I was given? That's right: I had to make the granola. And I couldn't believe how easy it was! After that, I felt like I'd missed *years* of granola making. (I've since made up for it by baking a fresh batch of granola every week. I think I've almost caught up.)

So don't be afraid. As you look through the base recipe and variations, you'll probably notice two things: I like to keep my granola ingredients simple, and I don't add dried fruit. It's not that I have anything against dried fruit; I've just found I prefer my granola without it. So feel free to toss your favorite dried fruits—such as apricots or cranberries—into the still-warm granola, if you like.

Also, I love using different types of grains in homemade granola. And they're not difficult to find; most natural food stores sell a variety of grains that have been pressed into flakes. A few of my favorites include rye, kamut, spelt, and barley. Use them on their own in place of the oats, alongside the oats, or come up with your own custom-made multigrain mix.

All-Natural Granola

YIELD: 3 CUPS (440 G)

· ·

2 cups (200 g) rolled oats
1 cup (110 g) pecan pieces
⅛ teaspoon sea salt
¼ cup (60 ml) maple syrup
¼ cup (60 ml) walnut oil
½ teaspoon vanilla extract

To make the granola: Preheat the oven to 300˚F (150˚C, or gas mark 2). In a bowl, toss together the oats, pecans, and salt. In a separate bowl, whisk together the maple syrup, walnut oil, and vanilla extract. Pour into the oat mixture and stir until the oats are well coated.

Spread the oats on a baking sheet and cover with wax paper. Using your hands or a rolling pin, press down on the granola to spread it evenly across the baking sheet. Remove the wax paper. Bake for 40 to 50 minutes, rotating the pan halfway through baking. The granola should be golden and starting to brown around the edges. Remove the pan from the oven and let cool completely on the pan.

Once the granola is cool, break it into pieces and store in an airtight container at room temperature for up to a week.

 Stay away from coated or dark-colored sheet trays: they'll brown the bottom of your granola too quickly.

SPRING

Roasted Strawberries with Almond-Kamut

YIELD: 2 GRANOLA PARFAITS, 3 CUPS (440 G) GRANOLA

1 recipe All-Natural Granola (page 24)
1 cup (100 g) Kamut flakes
1 cup (100 g) sliced almonds

Parfait

2 cups (280 g) quartered strawberries
2 teaspoons honey
2 cups (480 g) plain whole-milk yogurt or Greek-style yogurt

Make the granola recipe as directed using the Kamut flakes in place of 1 cup (100 g) of the oats and the almonds in place of the pecans.

To make the parfait: Preheat the oven to 375°F (190°C, or gas mark 5). Spread the strawberries in a roasting pan and bake for 20 minutes. Toss with the honey and let cool. Swirl the roasted strawberries into the yogurt. Divide among 2 bowls and finish with ¼ cup (36 g) of granola for each bowl.

 SUMMER

Ginger Blueberries with Honey

YIELD: 2 GRANOLA PARFAITS, 3 CUPS (440 G) GRANOLA

1 recipe All-Natural Granola (page 24)
½ cup (85 g) uncooked quinoa
¼ cup (80 g) honey

Parfait

3 cups (360 g) blueberries
1 tablespoon (20 g) honey
1 tablespoon (15 ml) lemon juice
2 teaspoons minced ginger
2 teaspoons lemon zest
2 cups (480 g) plain whole-milk yogurt or Greek-style yogurt

Preheat the oven to 250°F (120°C, or gas mark ½). Rinse (and soak, if desired) the quinoa, and spread out in a thin layer on a baking tray covered with parchment paper. Bake until the liquid has evaporated, 15 to 20 minutes.

Make the granola recipe as directed, replacing the maple syrup with the honey and using the quinoa in place of the pecans.

To make the parfait: Place the blueberries in a small saucepan along with the honey, lemon juice, ginger, and lemon zest. Heat over medium-low heat until the blueberries are juicy, 5 to 6 minutes. Remove from the heat and let cool. Swirl the blueberries into the yogurt. Divide among 2 bowls and finish with ¼ cup (36 g) of granola for each bowl.

FALL

Cinnamon Apples with Sorghum-Spelt

YIELD: 2 GRANOLA PARFAITS, 3 CUPS (440 G) GRANOLA

. . . .

1 recipe All-Natural Granola (page 24)
2 cups (200 g) rolled spelt flakes
¼ cup (80 g) sorghum syrup

Parfait

1 tablespoon (14 g) butter
1 large apple, peeled, cored, and cut into ¼-inch (6 mm) cubes
1 teaspoon cinnamon
1 tablespoon (15 ml) maple syrup
2 cups (480 g) plain whole-milk yogurt or Greek-style yogurt

Make the granola as directed, using the spelt flakes in place of the oats and the sorghum in place of the maple syrup.

To make the parfait: Melt the butter in a skillet over low heat. Add the apple, cinnamon, and maple syrup. Cook until the apples are soft, 5 to 6 minutes. Remove from the heat and let cool. Divide the yogurt among 2 bowls and top with the apples and 3 to 4 tablespoons (27 to 36 g) of the spelt granola.

 WINTER

Pomegranate and Hazelnut

YIELD: 2 GRANOLA PARFAITS, 3 CUPS (440 G) GRANOLA

. . . .

1 recipe All-Natural Granola (page 24)
1 cup (100 g) crushed hazelnuts, skins on
½ teaspoon cardamom powder

Parfait

½ cup (120 ml) pomegranate juice
1 tablespoon (20 g) honey
2 cups (480 g) plain whole-milk yogurt or Greek yogurt
¼ cup (40 g) pomegranate arils

Make the granola as directed, using the hazelnuts in place of the pecans and adding the cardamom to the dry mixture.

To make the parfait: In a small saucepan, whisk together the pomegranate juice and honey. Bring to a boil, reduce the heat to medium-low, and let the pomegranate juice cook down until it reduces by half, 5 to 6 minutes. Let cool. Swirl the pomegranate juice mixture into the yogurt. Divide among 2 bowls and finish with ¼ cup (36 g) of the granola and 2 tablespoons (20 g) pomegranate arils for each bowl.

Waffles and Toppings

When I was growing up, our on-the-go family relied heavily on prepackaged frozen foods. Somewhere along the line, I got the idea that the frozen meals I was eating were versions of foods that were difficult to make at home, and waffles fell into that category. When I moved away from processed foods, though, I finally tried making them at home, and I couldn't believe how easy it was. Sure, I'd eaten frozen waffles for years, but once I found out how easy it was to whip up waffles at home, I never looked back.

Now homemade waffles are one of our favorite weekend breakfasts. My husband and I top ours with butter, a handful of fresh fruit, and a drizzle of good maple syrup. (Of course, we enjoy the occasional guilty pleasure, too. My husband likes to sneak a scoop of ice cream on top of his waffles, while I add a dollop of freshly whipped cream.)

Go ahead and experiment with different flours when you're making waffles. Oat flour works well, as in the fall variation, but it's also fun to combine a few different flours, such as wheat and rye, for a multigrain version. Do use whole milk, if you can: A little extra fat means a crispier waffle. (If you'd rather use nondairy milk, no problem. Just add 1 to 2 tablespoons [14 to 28 g] more of melted butter, and decrease the milk by the same amount.)

Whole Wheat Waffles

YIELD: 4 WAFFLES

. . . .

1½ cups (180 g) whole wheat pastry or
   unbleached all-purpose flour
2 teaspoons baking powder
½ teaspoon sea salt
1 cup (240 ml) whole milk
2 large eggs
4 tablespoons (56 g) melted butter
1 tablespoon (15 ml) maple syrup
½ teaspoon vanilla extract

Preheat the waffle iron. In a bowl, whisk together the flour, baking powder, and sea salt. In a separate bowl, whisk together the milk, eggs, melted butter, maple syrup, and vanilla extract. Pour the wet ingredients into the dry and stir until combined but with a few lumps, being careful not to overmix.

Pour a quarter of the batter into the waffle iron and cook per the waffle iron directions. Keep finished waffles on a baking tray in a 200°F (93°C) oven until ready to serve. Serve with butter, maple syrup, fruit, and/or whipped cream.

SPRING

Cheddar Waffles with Roasted Radishes and Fried Eggs

YIELD: 4 SERVINGS

. . . .

1 recipe Whole Wheat Waffles (page 27)
2 bunches radishes
2 tablespoons (30 ml) olive oil, divided
½ teaspoon sea salt
¼ teaspoon black pepper
1 cup (120 g) shredded sharp Cheddar cheese
4 eggs

Preheat the oven to 400°F (200°C, or gas mark 6). Quarter the radishes and toss with 1 tablespoon (15 ml) of the olive oil, salt, and black pepper. Spread in a thin layer in a roasting pan and bake for 22 to 25 minutes, until tender but still slightly crisp.

Make the waffles as directed, adding the Cheddar to the wet ingredients.

When ready to serve, heat a skillet or griddle over medium-low heat and add the remaining 1 tablespoon (15 ml) olive oil. Crack the eggs into the skillet and fry over-easy, 2 to 3 minutes on each side.

Serve the waffles with a healthy scoop of radishes and 1 egg.

 SUMMER

Rye Waffles with Lemon and Blackberries

YIELD: 4 SERVINGS

. . . .

1 recipe Whole Wheat Waffles (page 27)
4 cups (560 g) blackberries
2 tablespoons (30 ml) maple syrup
1 tablespoon (15 ml) lemon juice
1 teaspoon lemon zest
1 cup (120 g) rye flour

In a blender, combine the blackberries with the maple syrup, lemon juice, and lemon zest. Pulse 2 or 3 times to break down the blackberries. Pour into a bowl and set aside.

Make the waffles as directed using the rye flour in place of 1 cup (120 g) of the wheat flour.

Serve the waffles with the blackberries and extra maple syrup.

FALL

Oat Waffles with Maple-Cardamom Plums

YIELD: 4 SERVINGS

• •

1 recipe Whole Wheat Waffles (page 27)
½ cup (50 g) oat flour
½ cup (50 g) old-fashioned rolled oats
¼ cup (60 ml) maple syrup
¾ pound (340 g) plums, thinly sliced
⅛ teaspoon cardamom

Make the waffles as directed using the oat flour and rolled oats in place of ½ cup of the wheat flour and increase the milk amount by 2 tablespoons (30 ml).

Heat the maple syrup in a pan over medium-low heat. Add the plums and cardamom, and cook until the plums are tender, 5 to 6 minutes. Spoon the plums onto the waffles and serve with extra maple syrup if desired.

 WINTER

Cornbread Waffles with Roasted Grapefruit

YIELD: 4 SERVINGS

• •

1 recipe Whole Wheat Waffles (page 27)
¾ cup (90 g) fine cornmeal
1 grapefruit
2 tablespoons (30 g) sucanat

Preheat the oven to 425°F (220°C, or gas mark 7). Make the waffles as directed, replacing ¾ cup (90 g) of the wheat flour with the cornmeal.

Slice the skin off the grapefruit and cut into slices. Place in a roasting pan and sprinkle with the sucanat. Bake for 15 to 20 minutes, until the sugar has caramelized and is lightly browned. Serve on top of the waffles.

Omelet

If I only got to choose a single breakfast recipe to share with you, it'd be the omelet. It's as simple as it gets in terms of ingredients, but once you start adding herbs, cheeses, and produce, the combinations are nearly endless. Plus, omelets cook up quickly, and the best part is it's essentially foolproof. Even when you mess up, you'll still have a delicious dish of scrambled eggs to enjoy!

Invest in a couple of key tools before making omelets at home. Get a good nonstick 8-inch (20 cm) skillet and a small spatula. Lots of stores sell nonstick pans made from ceramic that are certified safe at all temperatures. They might be a bit pricier than the traditional skillet, but they work so well that I highly recommend investing in one for omelet making (and for making the crepes on page 168).

If you prefer an egg-white omelet, simply replace the eggs in this recipe with 3 or 4 egg whites, and continue with the recipe as directed. And don't stop with the mixed herbs listed in the basic recipe. Depending on the season, dill, sage, marjoram, cilantro, and fennel are all great additions. In fact, making omelets at home gave me a great reason to start a patio herb garden so that I'd have plenty of fresh herbs at my fingertips.

Herbed Omelet

YIELD: 1 OMELET

. . . .

1½ teaspoons (7 g) butter
2 large or extra-large eggs
2 tablespoons (30 ml) whole milk
1 tablespoon (4 g) mixed chopped fresh herbs: basil, thyme, rosemary, and/or parsley
⅛ teaspoon salt
⅛ teaspoon black pepper
½ to 1 tablespoon (4 to 8 g) shredded cheese (optional)

Melt the butter in a nonstick 8-inch (20 cm) pan over low heat. In a bowl, whisk together the eggs, milk, fresh herbs, salt, and pepper until the eggs are slightly lighter in color and a bit frothy. Once the butter has melted, swirl around the pan to evenly cover the bottom.

Pour the egg mixture into the skillet. Let the eggs set around the edges, 30 to 60 seconds. Then with a spatula, run along the edges, lifting the set egg and letting egg run under. Continue to do this until the majority of the omelet is set.

Add the cheese (or other filling ingredients) on one half. Fold the empty half of the omelet over and continue to cook for 1 to 2 minutes more. Flip and continue to cook for 1 to 2 minutes. The filling should be set. Flip the omelet onto a plate to serve. Repeat for as many omelets as needed.

Green Chile, Onion, and Avocado Herbed Omelet >

SPRING

Chard, Green Garlic, and Mozzarella

YIELD: 1 OMELET

. . . .

1 recipe Herbed Omelet (page 30)
1 teaspoon olive oil
½ tablespoon (5 g) minced green garlic
½ cup (20 g) packed Swiss chard leaves, julienned
1 tablespoon (10 g) fresh mozzarella cheese

In an 8-inch (20 cm) skillet, heat the olive oil over medium-low heat. Add the green garlic and cook until fragrant and tender, 2 to 3 minutes. Stir in the Swiss chard and cook for 1 to 2 minutes, until slightly wilted. Remove from the skillet and set aside.

Make the omelet as directed, using the chard and mozzarella cheese as the filling.

 SUMMER

Green Chile, Onion, and Avocado

YIELD: 1 OMELET

. . . .

1 recipe Herbed Omelet (page 30)
1 teaspoon olive oil
½ Hatch green chile, diced
1½ tablespoons (15 g) minced red onion
1 tablespoon (1 g) cilantro
1 tablespoon (4 g) Cheddar cheese
½ ripe avocado, sliced, for serving

In an 8-inch (20 cm) skillet, heat the olive oil over medium-low heat. Add the chile and onion and sauté until tender, 7 to 8 minutes. Transfer to a bowl and stir in the cilantro.

Make the omelet as directed, using the chile-onion mixture and cheese as the filling. Serve with the sliced avocado.

FALL

Shredded Brussels Sprouts and Havarti Cheese

YIELD: 1 OMELET

• •

1 recipe Herbed Omelet (page 30)
1 teaspoon olive oil
2 tablespoons (12 g) thinly sliced leek
2 ounces (54 g) raw shredded Brussels sprouts
1 tablespoon (7 g) shredded Havarti cheese

In an 8-inch (20 cm) skillet, heat the olive oil over medium-low heat. Add the leeks and sauté until tender, 3 to 4 minutes. Add the Brussels sprouts and continue to cook until tender, another 3 to 4 minutes. Transfer to a bowl and set aside.

Make the omelet as directed, using the Brussels sprout mixture and Havarti as the filling.

 Cooking the sprouts in oil gives them a slight crispness. If tender, soft Brussels sprouts are desired, add 1 to 2 teaspoons of water to the pan along with the sprouts, and cook until soft.

 WINTER

Fennel, Black Olive, and Feta

YIELD: 1 OMELET

• •

1 recipe Herbed Omelet (page 30)
1 teaspoon unsalted butter
2 tablespoons (12 g) sliced red onion
2½ tablespoons (15 g) thinly sliced fennel
⅛ teaspoon fresh minced thyme
1 tablespoon (10 g) sliced pitted black olives
1½ teaspoons feta cheese

Melt the butter in an 8-inch (20 cm) skillet over low heat. Add the onion and cook for 3 to 4 minutes, until tender. Stir in the fennel and cook for another 4 to 5 minutes, until starting to brown. Stir in the thyme, then transfer to a bowl and toss with the sliced black olives.

Make the omelet as directed, using the fennel mixture and feta as the filling.

Scones

I dreamed of opening my own bakery for years. When I graduated from college, I got a job at a bakery as counter help, and that eventually led to a full-time job as a baker. I absorbed everything I possibly could, and kept that valuable knowledge tucked away in a corner of my brain when I headed back to grad school. After grad school, I had my eye on a local coffee shop that I hoped to buy and upgrade into a bakery. That didn't work out, but the upside was, I had a substantial stockpile of tested recipes I was planning on using in my bakery, and these scones were high up on that list.

My qualifications for a good scone? Firm on the outside, soft on the inside, and just sweet enough to get the point across. That's pretty specific, but it's for a good reason, because I've had my fair share of disappointing scones with soggy textures and little-to-no flavor. It's true that these scones aren't the healthiest item in my repertoire, but cutting back on the butter and heavy cream in the recipe yields scones that are only so-so. So this scone recipe is my once-in-a-while treat, and I especially like to make them when I have a little leftover fresh fruit to add to the mix.

Like my muffin recipe on page 21, these scones can be made ahead of time and frozen. (If you're using fresh fruit in them, I recommend freezing the fruit before adding it to the batter, as freezing helps the fruit from "running" and making a mess.) Again, it's best to resist the temptation to cut back on the butter or to cut out the heavy cream. Just remember—everything in moderation!

Cream Scones

YIELD: 8 SCONES

. . . .

2¼ cups (270 g) whole wheat pastry flour or
    unbleached all-purpose flour
2 teaspoons baking powder
¼ teaspoon sea salt
½ cup (112 g) unsalted butter, chilled and cubed
1 large egg
½ cup (120 ml) heavy cream, divided
⅓ cup (80 ml) maple syrup
1 teaspoon vanilla extract
1½ cups (225 g) chopped fruit, chocolate chips,
    or a combination of both

Preheat the oven to 425°F (220°C, or gas mark 7). Cover a baking sheet with parchment paper.

Place the flour, baking powder, and salt in a food processor. Pulse until combined. Add the butter and pulse until the mixture is in small, pea-size pieces. Transfer to a large bowl.

In a separate bowl, whisk together the egg, 6 tablespoons (90 ml) of the heavy cream, maple syrup, and vanilla extract. Pour into the dry ingredients and stir until just combined.

Turn out the dough onto a floured surface and pat into a rough 12 by 6-inch (30 by 15 cm) rectangle. Sprinkle the chopped fruit over, and roll into a log, jelly-roll style. Squeeze and pat the log into a slightly flatter log, about 1 inch (2.5 cm) thick. Using a knife or bench scoop, cut into 8 squares or triangles.

Place the scones 1 to 2 inches (2.5 to 5 cm) apart on the baking sheet. Brush with the remaining heavy cream. Bake the scones until firm to the touch and golden, 18 to 20 minutes. Remove from the oven and transfer to a rack to cool. Store in an airtight container at room temperature for 2 to 3 days or freeze for extended storage.

Apricot and Strawberry

YIELD: 8 SCONES

. . . .

1 recipe Cream Scones (page 34)
¾ cup (120 g) diced fresh apricots
½ cup (65 g) quartered strawberries
1 vanilla bean, cut in half

Two to 3 hours before making the scones, place the apricots and strawberries in a bowl and place in the freezer. Once the fruit is frozen, make the scones as directed, scraping the vanilla bean seeds into the dry mixture and using the apricots and strawberries as the filling.

 SUMMER

Cherry Almond

YIELD: 8 SCONES

. . . .

1 recipe Cream Scones (page 34)
1 cup (140 g) pitted cherries, quartered
¼ cup (30 g) almond slices or pieces

Make the scones as directed, using the cherries and sliced almonds as the filling.

FALL

Butternut Squash, Blue Cheese, and Rosemary

YIELD: 8 SCONES

1 recipe Cream Scones (page 34)
2 cups (280 g) ¼-inch (6 mm) cubed butternut squash
1 tablespoon (15 ml) olive oil
2 ounces (54 g) blue cheese, crumbled
1 tablespoon (2 g) minced fresh rosemary

Before preparing the scones, preheat the oven to 425°F (220°C, or gas mark 7). Toss the squash with the olive oil and spread in a single layer in a roasting pan. Roast for 25 minutes, or until the squash is tender. Let cool completely.

Make the scones as directed, but stir together the roasted squash, blue cheese, and rosemary before adding the mixture to the wet ingredients.

 WINTER

Lemon-Poppy Seed

YIELD: 8 SCONES

1 recipe Cream Scones (page 34)
2 tablespoons (16 g) poppy seeds
2 tablespoons (12 g) lemon zest
3 tablespoons (45 ml) lemon juice

Icing
½ cup (60 g) confectioners' sugar
1 tablespoon (15 ml) lemon juice
1 teaspoon lemon zest

Make the scones as directed, adding the poppy seeds and lemon zest to the dry mixture and using the lemon juice in place of 3 tablespoons (45 ml) of the heavy cream.

To make the icing: Whisk together the confectioners' sugar, lemon juice, and lemon zest in a bowl. Once the scones have cooled slightly, spread roughly 1 teaspoon of icing on each one.

Porridge

For the longest time, porridge wasn't a part of my vocabulary (unless I happened to be reading a book it was featured in). As a child—and even into my twenties—I didn't eat oatmeal because of the weird, somewhat "goopy" texture. And I lumped porridge into the very same category. Horrified, I'd watch my father eat Cream of Wheat, and could never understand the appeal. No oatmeal, no porridge, no way.

But when I first began to introduce whole grains into my diet, I stumbled upon amaranth porridge by accident. I was experimenting with different grains, and when I cooked up amaranth, expecting it to be the consistency of rice, I got a lovely porridge instead. It messed up the meal I was making at the time, but great discoveries are often born of mistakes, and I ended up realizing that whole-grain porridges are a great way to play with a variety of grains (and flavors).

Some grains, such as teff and amaranth, work well as a creamy porridge without any modifications, while other grains, such as wheat grains or millet, need to be cracked to achieve a porridge-like consistency. (I keep a cheap coffee grinder on hand for the grain cracking.) Or, if you don't feel like cracking the grain, soaking the whole grains overnight will make for quicker cooking times, and will help unlock their nutrients. Try out a few different varieties, each grain has a different personality.

Grain Porridge

YIELD: 1 OR 2 SERVINGS

. . . .

½ cup (90 g) amaranth
1 cup (240 ml) water
2 tablespoons (30 ml) whole milk
2 teaspoons maple syrup
¼ teaspoon vanilla extract
⅛ teaspoon sea salt

Soak the amaranth overnight, if possible.

Drain and rinse the amaranth in cheesecloth. Combine with the water, milk, maple syrup, vanilla extract, and salt in a pot. Bring to a boil, and reduce to a simmer. Cover and let simmer for 15 minutes. Remove from the heat and let sit for 10 more minutes to thicken. Add a bit of milk or water to thin, if desired.

 To coax extra flavor from the grain, toast it in a dry skillet over medium heat for 2 to 3 minutes before soaking or cracking.

Quinoa Porridge with Cranberry

SPRING

Farro with Ginger Rhubarb

YIELD: 2 SERVINGS

. . . .

½ cup (90 g) farro
½ cup (55 g) diced rhubarb
¾ cup (180 ml) milk
¾ cup (180 ml) water
1 tablespoon (6 g) minced ginger
3 tablespoons (45 ml) maple syrup

Crack the farro in a blender or coffee grinder. Combine with all the ingredients in a small saucepan. Bring to a boil, reduce to a simmer, cover, and cook until the farro is tender, 35 to 40 minutes.

 SUMMER

Savory Millet with Tomato and Eggs

YIELD: 2 SERVINGS

. . . .

Porridge
½ cup (90 g) millet
1½ cups (360 ml) water
¼ teaspoon sea salt
½ cup (120 ml) whole milk
1 ounce (28 g) Cheddar cheese, grated

Topping
1 tablespoon (15 ml) olive oil
2 cups (280 g) cherry tomatoes
2 tablespoons (8 g) julienned basil
¼ teaspoon sea salt
¼ teaspoon black pepper
2 poached or fried eggs

To make the porridge: Add the millet to a pot over medium heat. Swirl for 2 to 3 minutes, letting the millet toast lightly. Add the water and salt, bring to a boil, reduce to a simmer, and cook until the water is absorbed, 25 to 30 minutes. Stir the millet occasionally as it cooks.

To make the topping: Heat the olive oil in a skillet over medium heat. Add the cherry tomatoes and cook until tender, stirring occasionally, 4 to 6 minutes. Use the back of a wooden spoon to burst the tomatoes once hot. Remove from the heat and stir in the basil, salt, and pepper.

Once the millet is done, remove from the heat and stir in the milk and cheese. Add more or less milk depending on the desired texture. Divide among 2 bowls and top each with the tomatoes and a poached egg.

FALL

Quinoa with Cranberry

YIELD: 2 OR 3 SERVINGS

. . . .

Quinoa
1 cup (180 g) quinoa
1 cup (240 ml) water
1½ cups (360 ml) whole milk
½ teaspoon vanilla extract

Cranberries
2 cups (220 g) fresh/frozen cranberries
1 cup (120 g) shredded apple
3 tablespoons (45 ml) maple syrup
½ teaspoon cinnamon
2 tablespoons (12 g) crushed pecans

To make the quinoa: Combine the quinoa ingredients in a small pot, bring to a boil, reduce to a simmer, and cover. Let cook for 12 to 14 minutes, until most of the liquid has been absorbed. Remove from the heat and let sit for another 5 minutes.

To make the cranberries: Combine the cranberries, apple, maple syrup, and cinnamon in another small pot. Heat over medium-low heat until the cranberries have released their juices, 5 to 6 minutes. Top the quinoa with the cranberry mixture and sprinkle with the crushed pecans.

 Even with the 3 tablespoons (45 ml) of maple syrup and the apples, the cranberries will still be a bit tart. If you want a sweeter porridge, add more maple syrup.

 WINTER

Buckwheat with Maple Sweet Potato

YIELD: 2 OR 3 SERVINGS

. . . .

Kasha
1 cup (240 ml) water
1 cup (240 ml) milk, plus extra for serving
1 cup (160 g) kasha (roasted buckwheat)
¼ teaspoon sea salt

Topping
2 cups (240 g) ½-inch (1.3 cm) peeled and cubed sweet potato
2 tablespoons (30 ml) maple syrup
1 tablespoon (14 g) butter
½ teaspoon cinnamon
2 to 3 tablespoons (15 to 23 g) crushed walnuts

To make the kasha: Bring the water and milk to a near boil in a saucepan and stir in the kasha and salt. Cook for 12 to 15 minutes, until tender and most of the liquid has been absorbed.

To make the topping: Steam the sweet potato cubes until just tender, 7 to 8 minutes. Place in a bowl and toss with the maple syrup, butter, and cinnamon, letting the butter melt. Stir the sweet potatoes into the kasha porridge and serve with a sprinkle of crushed walnuts and a splash of milk.

 I typically use roasted buckwheat, but raw buckwheat will work as well if you prefer a more subdued flavor

Quiche

Although I've placed quiche in the breakfast chapter, the truth is, it's good for any meal. Served with a salad, quiche makes a nice, light but filling lunch or dinner. And, much like the frittata on page 17, it makes a solid base for just about any type of ingredient you have on hand.

The main difference between a quiche and a frittata is, obviously, the crust. I grew up on vegetable oil crust, but since I ditched the trans fats, I prefer a butter-and-cream-cheese crust (another combination I picked up from my quiche-making aunt!). And they're great for making ahead. If you're planning on serving one at breakfast or brunch, you can assemble the quiche the night before and bake it in the morning. Quiche also keeps well, covered and in the refrigerator, for several days, so there's no danger of leftovers going to waste.

Cream Cheese Quiche

YIELD: 8 TO 10 SERVINGS

. . . .

Crust
1¼ cups (150 g) unbleached all-purpose flour
   or whole wheat pastry flour
¼ teaspoon sea salt
6 tablespoons (84 g) cold unsalted butter
1 ounce (28 g) cream cheese
3 tablespoons (45 ml) cold water
1 tablespoon (15 ml) maple syrup

Filling
8 large or extra-large eggs
2½ cups (600 ml) whole milk
½ teaspoon sea salt
½ teaspoon black pepper
4 ounces (112 g) cheese, shredded

To make the crust: Combine the flour and salt in a bowl and cut in the butter and cream cheese with your fingers (or a pastry blender). Once the butter is broken down to the size of peas, add the water and maple syrup and stir and knead until the dough comes together. Turn out onto a floured work surface and gather into a disc. Wrap with plastic wrap and place in the refrigerator for 20 minutes to chill.

Preheat the oven to 425°F (220°C, or gas mark 7). Roll out the dough and crimp into an 11-inch (28 cm) quiche pan or a 9-inch (23 cm) pie pan. Parbake the crust for 10 to 15 minutes, until lightly golden. Remove from the oven and set aside on a baking tray. Reduce the oven to 375°F (190°C, or gas mark 5).

To make the filling: Whisk together the eggs, milk, salt, and pepper in a large bowl. If you're using other fillings, spread them in a layer over the crust, and pour the egg mixture over. Sprinkle with the shredded cheese. Bake until the eggs have set and puffed, 45 to 55 minutes. Remove from the oven and cool for 10 to 15 minutes before serving.

To reheat the quiche, cover with foil and bake for 18 to 20 minutes in a 325°F (170°C, or gas mark 3) oven.

SPRING

Scallion with Pea Shoot Salad

YIELD: 8 TO 10 SERVINGS

. . . .

1 recipe Cream Cheese Quiche (page 40)
1 bunch scallions, minced
1 medium shallot, minced
¼ cup (12 g) minced chives
4 ounces (112 g) fontina cheese, shredded

Salad
2 cups (40 g) pea shoots
2 tablespoons (12 g) toasted pine nuts
1 tablespoon (15 ml) olive oil
2 teaspoons lemon juice
2 teaspoons honey
¼ teaspoon sea salt
¼ teaspoon black pepper

In a small bowl, combine the scallions, shallot, and chives. Make the quiche as directed, spreading the scallion mixture over the crust before filling and sprinkling the top with the fontina cheese.

To make the salad: While the quiche bakes, combine the pea shoots and pine nuts in a bowl. In a separate bowl, whisk together the olive oil, lemon juice, honey, salt, and pepper. Pour over the pea shoots and toss until coated. When ready to serve, sprinkle the salad over the quiche.

 SUMMER

Potato Hash

YIELD: 8 TO 10 SERVINGS

. . . .

1 recipe Cream Cheese Quiche (page 40)
2 cups (220 g) ¼-inch (6 mm) cubed red potatoes
½ red pepper, seeded and diced
½ medium red onion, diced
1 tablespoon (15 ml) olive oil
½ teaspoon sea salt
¼ teaspoon black pepper
1 tablespoon (2 g) minced fresh rosemary
3 ounces (84 g) goat cheese

Preheat the oven to 425°F (220°C, or gas mark 7).

Toss the red potatoes, red pepper, and onion with the olive oil, sea salt, and black pepper. Spread the mixture in a roasting pan or on a parchment-covered baking sheet. Roast until the potatoes are lightly browned and cooked, 35 to 40 minutes. Let cool.

Make the quiche as directed, using the red potato mixture as the filling and whisking the minced rosemary into the egg mixture. Sprinkle the goat cheese on top before baking.

Broccoli-Cheddar Quiche

 FALL

Broccoli-Cheddar

YIELD: 8 TO 10 SERVINGS

. . . .

1 recipe Cream Cheese Quiche (page 40)
2 cups (140 g) broccoli florets
2 cloves garlic, minced
1 tablespoon (4 g) minced flat-leaf parsley
4 ounces (112 g) Cheddar cheese

Place a steam basket in a pot with a small amount of water. Add the broccoli, bring the water to a boil, and steam the broccoli until tender, 3 to 4 minutes. Transfer to a bowl and toss with the garlic and parsley.

Make the quiche as directed, adding the steamed broccoli and Cheddar to the filling.

 WINTER

Spicy Kale

YIELD: 8 TO 10 SERVINGS

. . . .

1 recipe Cream Cheese Quiche (page 40)
1 tablespoon (15 ml) olive oil
½ medium yellow onion, minced
2 cups (80 g) packed shredded dinosaur kale
½ teaspoon red pepper flakes
2 tablespoons (30 ml) water
4 ounces (112 g) shredded Havarti cheese

Heat a skillet over medium-low heat. Add the olive oil, then the onion. Cook, stirring occasionally, until fragrant and translucent, 5 to 6 minutes. Add the shredded kale, red pepper flakes, and water. Cover and cook for about 1 to 2 minutes, until wilted.

Make the quiche as directed, adding the cooked kale and Havarti to the filling.

Dutch Baby

My husband and I have a weekend tradition: each Saturday, we pick a new location to visit, or a new activity to try. This tradition usually means we eat breakfast out, because there's nothing we love more than long weekend brunches. Our typical weekday breakfasts involve eggs, granola, or oatmeal, but on weekends, we indulge in waffles or a Dutch baby, topped with a scoop of fresh fruit.

In case you've never heard of it before, a Dutch baby is a type of pancake that puffs up in the oven and, once removed, settles down into a dense meal. They're super-easy to make. In fact, I tend to make Dutch babies more often than waffles or pancakes, because you can just stick them in the oven, walk away, and in roughly 20 minutes you've got a meal that serves three or four people. It might look complicated, but it's not, and it's fun to watch a Dutch baby bake.

Lemon Blackberry Einkorn Dutch Baby

Although using pastry flour will keep your Dutch baby light and puffy during baking, I encourage you to play around with different types of flour, such as rye or oat. One caveat, though: don't add toppings to it until it's out of the oven, because toppings or fillings will keep it from rising. (The one exception to that rule is my savory spring variation, a multigrain herbed-pea Dutch baby.)

Delicious Dutch Baby

YIELD: 3 TO 4 SERVINGS

. . . .

½ cup plus 2 tablespoons (75 g) whole wheat pastry flour or unbleached all-purpose flour
½ cup (120 ml) whole milk
2 large eggs
2 tablespoons (30 ml) maple syrup
1 teaspoon lemon zest
½ teaspoon vanilla extract
⅛ teaspoon sea salt
1 tablespoon (14 g) unsalted butter

Preheat the oven to 400°F (200°C, or gas mark 6).

Combine the flour, milk, eggs, maple syrup, lemon zest, vanilla extract, and sea salt in a blender. Puree for 10 to 15 seconds, until well combined.

Melt the butter in an 8-inch (20 cm) cast-iron (well-seasoned) skillet. Swirl around to cover the pan once melted. Remove from the heat and pour in the batter. Place the skillet in the oven and bake until golden brown and puffed, 22 to 25 minutes.

💬 *The Dutch baby can also be made in a 10-inch (25 cm) oven-safe skillet. Simply reduce the cooking time to 18 to 20 minutes.*

Multigrain Herbed Pea

YIELD: 3 TO 4 SERVINGS

. . . .

1 recipe Delicious Dutch Baby (page 43)
3 tablespoons (22 g) rye flour
3 tablespoons (18 g) oat flour
¼ cup (30 g) whole wheat pastry flour
½ cup (75 g) shelled peas
¼ cup (24 g) chopped scallion
1 ounce (28 g) shredded white Cheddar cheese

Make the Dutch baby as directed, using the flour mixture listed above in place of the ½ cup plus 2 tablespoons (75 g) pastry flour. After pouring the Dutch baby mixture into the prepared skillet, sprinkle with the peas, scallion, and cheese.

 Filling the Dutch baby will keep it from rising. Alternatively, cook the peas and scallions in a bit of olive oil and spoon over the cooked Dutch baby.

Lemon Blackberry Einkorn

YIELD: 3 TO 4 SERVINGS

. . . .

1 recipe Delicious Dutch Baby (page 43)
¾ cup (76 g) einkorn flour
2 cups (240 g) blackberries
2 tablespoons (30 ml) maple syrup
1 teaspoon lemon zest

Make the Dutch baby as directed, using the einkorn flour in place of the whole wheat pastry flour. While the Dutch baby is baking, combine the berries, maple syrup, and lemon zest in a saucepan. Heat the mixture, smashing the blackberries with the back of a fork, until warm, 3 to 4 minutes. Top the freshly baked Dutch baby with the blackberry mixture.

FALL

Pecan Pear

YIELD: 3 TO 4 SERVINGS

. . . .

1 recipe Delicious Dutch Baby (page 43)
¼ cup (25 g) pecan meal
1 tablespoon (14 g) unsalted butter
1 pear, peeled and cubed
1 tablespoon (20 g) honey
1 tablespoon (15 ml) heavy cream
Sprinkle of cinnamon, for serving

Make the Dutch baby as directed, adding the pecan meal to the batter. While Dutch baby bakes, melt the butter in a skillet over low heat. Add the cubed pear and honey. Cook over low heat for 10 minutes, until the pears are tender. Stir in the heavy cream. Top the freshly baked Dutch baby with the cooked pear mixture and a sprinkle of cinnamon.

 WINTER

Coconut Kiwi

YIELD: 3 TO 4 SERVINGS

. . . .

1 recipe Delicious Dutch Baby (page 43)
1 tablespoon (6 g) orange zest, divided
3 kiwis, peeled and cubed
3 tablespoons (12 g) unsweetened coconut flakes
1 tablespoon (15 ml) orange juice
Honey, for serving

Make the Dutch baby as directed, adding 2 teaspoons (4 g) of the orange zest to the batter. While the Dutch baby is baking, toss together the cubed kiwis, coconut flakes, orange juice, and remaining 1 teaspoon (2 g) orange zest. Top the freshly baked Dutch baby with the kiwi compote and a drizzle of honey.

 For this version, I like to use a drizzle of honey instead of the usual maple syrup.

3

Lunch/Light Dinners

I'm definitely a morning person and love breakfast, but if I had to choose an all-time favorite meal, it'd be lunch. And when I can, I try to make lunch my largest meal of the day. It keeps my energy levels up, and also gives my body plenty of time to digest. I'd much rather eat a big, rich meal at lunch than at dinner—although that, of course, isn't always easy during the workday, when I'm juggling a dozen projects at once.

When I worked in an office, I tried to make sure that lunchtime was an oasis of peace in the middle of a busy, chaotic day. And it usually worked. Sometimes I'd eat at my desk, but for the most part, I'd leave my desk—and I always made sure to take a full hour-long break. But eating lunch out every day quickly gets expensive, so I soon came up with recipes for meals that were easy to make in large batches. That way, I could eat portions of healthy, homemade food at lunchtime throughout the week.

Many of the recipes in this section also double as light dinners, and the leftovers are great for lunch over the next few days. Although the recipes here make relatively small yields, simply double a recipe if you want to have plenty left for weekday lunches. Give it a try, because a little planning ahead eliminates guesswork. You'll be much more likely to eat a sensible, filling lunch if you don't have to frantically whip something up before you rush out the door in the morning.

< Grilled Panzanella Salad with Burst Tomatoes

Soba Noodle Bowl

Everyone should have a few "clean-out-your-fridge" recipes in their repertoire—ones that use up the bits and pieces in the refrigerator or cupboard. I sure do. The day before I head to the grocery store, I'll sauté or roast last week's straggling vegetables, and toss them with noodles and peanut sauce, or with nothing more than a mixture of garlic, ginger, and soy sauce. It's hard to go wrong with such a simple combination, plus I usually end up with enough leftovers for a couple of days' worth of lunches.

That's where soba noodle bowls come in. I love using soba noodles in the recipes in this section, but I also keep a healthy stock of udon and brown rice noodles in the cupboard in case I'm in the mood for something different, and so should you. Soba noodles are typically made with a mix of buckwheat and wheat flour (but gluten-free versions can be found in specialty stores). The buckwheat flour lends them a nice nutty flavor, but if you aren't a fan, try replacing them with udon noodles. Their texture is similar, but because udon noodles are made strictly from wheat flour, their flavor is less imposing. Any of these recipes can easily be made gluten-free by substituting brown rice noodles (which are also handy for making spring rolls, page 93).

The sky's the limit when it comes to sauce options, but I have a weakness for peanut sauce. That said, other nut and seed butters can be used in place of the peanut butter, so feel free to substitute your favorite.

Simple Soba Bowl

YIELD: 2 SERVINGS

4 ounces (112 g) soba noodles
2 tablespoons (16 g) toasted sesame seeds
2 to 3 cups (300 to 450 g) cooked vegetables

Peanut Sauce
2 tablespoons (32 g) smooth peanut butter
¼ cup (60 ml) vegetable broth or water (only if cooking)
1 tablespoon (20 g) honey
½ teaspoon minced ginger
¼ teaspoon garlic powder
2 tablespoons (30 ml) tamari or soy sauce
½ tablespoon lime juice
⅛ teaspoon red pepper flakes (optional)

Bring a pot of water to a boil and add the noodles; cook until tender, 5 to 6 minutes. Drain, rinse, and place the noodles in a bowl. Add the sesame seeds and vegetables.

To make the peanut sauce: In a small bowl, whisk together all the ingredients. Pour into a saucepan and heat over low heat until warm and slightly thickened. Taste and adjust the flavors. Pour over the soba noodles and toss until well combined.

 If you're in a hurry and don't have time to cook the vegetables separately, just toss them with 1 tablespoon (15 ml) olive oil and roast at 425˚F (220˚C, or gas mark 7) until tender, 20 to 25 minutes. Also, to save time, don't heat the peanut sauce: just reduce the amount of vegetable broth or water to 2 tablespoons (30 ml).

SPRING

Roasted Snow Peas with Peanut Sauce

YIELD: 2 SERVINGS

. . . .

1 recipe Simple Soba Bowl (page 48)
2 cups (180 g) snow peas
1 clove garlic, minced
1 tablespoon (8 g) sesame seeds
1 tablespoon (15 ml) olive oil

Preheat the oven to 425°F (220°C, or gas mark 7). In a roasting pan, toss the snow peas, garlic, sesame seeds, and olive oil together. Spread in a thin layer and roast for 15 minutes. Stir and roast the mixture for another 10 to 15 minutes, until the snow peas are blistering.

Make the Simple Soba Bowl as directed, tossing the roasted snow peas with the noodles and sauce.

 Substitute sugar snap peas for the snow peas, if you like; choose whatever looks good at the farmers' market.

 SUMMER

Zucchini with Tahini Sauce

YIELD: 2 SERVINGS

. . . .

1 recipe Simple Soba Bowl (page 48)
1 medium zucchini
½ teaspoon sea salt
¼ cup (25 g) diced scallion (save the green parts for garnish)
2 tablespoons (30 g) tahini
Chopped cilantro, for topping
Lime wedges, for serving

Using a julienne peeler, slice the zucchini into "noodles." Toss them with the salt in a bowl, and allow to sit for 20 minutes. Transfer to a colander and squeeze the liquid out of them.

Make the Simple Soba Bowl as directed, tossing the zucchini noodles and scallion with the soba noodles and using tahini instead of peanut butter in the sauce. Add to the noodles, toss until well coated, and garnish with extra diced scallions, cilantro, and lime wedges.

Cabbage with Soy-Sesame Sauce

YIELD: 2 SERVINGS

. . . .

Noodle Bowl
1 tablespoon (15 ml) sesame oil
1 shallot, thinly sliced
4 cups (300 g) shredded red cabbage
4 ounces (112 g) soba noodles

Sauce
½ cup (120 ml) coconut milk
¼ cup (60 ml) vegetable broth
2 tablespoons (30 ml) soy sauce
2 teaspoons minced fresh ginger
1 tablespoon (20 g) honey
2 tablespoons (16 g) toasted sesame seeds
2 tablespoons (2 g) minced cilantro

To make the noodle bowl: Heat the sesame oil over medium-low heat in a large skillet. Add the shallot, cook for 2 to 3 minutes, and then add the cabbage, cooking for another 4 to 5 minutes. Bring a pot of water to a boil and add the noodles; cook until tender, 5 to 6 minutes. Drain, rinse, and set aside.

To make the sauce: Whisk together the sauce ingredients and add to the cabbage mixture. Turn the heat to low, cover, and let simmer until the cabbage is tender, 8 to 10 minutes. Remove from the heat and stir in the noodles. Top with the toasted sesame seeds and cilantro.

 I like to use red cabbage because of its color and slightly earthy flavor, but green, napa, or savoy cabbage would work just as well.

Shredded Brussels Sprouts with Ginger Sauce

YIELD: 2 SERVINGS

. . . .

Sauce
2 tablespoons (30 ml) tamari
2 tablespoons (30 ml) mirin
2 teaspoons honey
2 tablespoons (30 ml) pomegranate juice
1 clove garlic, minced
2 teaspoons (4 g) minced fresh ginger

Noodle Bowl
1 tablespoon (15 ml) olive oil
½ small red onion, thinly sliced
8 ounces (225 g) Brussels sprouts, shredded
3 tablespoons (45 ml) water
4 ounces (112 g) soba noodles
1 tablespoon (8 g) sesame seeds, for topping

To make the sauce: Whisk together all the ingredients for the sauce and set aside.

To make the noodle bowl: In a large skillet, heat the olive oil over medium-low heat. Add the onion and cook for 4 minutes. Stir in the Brussels sprouts and water. Cover and cook for 6 to 7 minutes, until the Brussels sprouts are bright green. Remove the lid and add the sauce. Turn the heat to low and simmer for 3 to 4 minutes, until the Brussels sprouts are tender.

Bring a pot of water to a boil and add the noodles; cook until tender, 5 to 6 minutes. Drain, rinse, and add to the Brussels sprouts. Serve with a sprinkle of sesame seeds.

 This dish isn't very heavy on the sauce, so if you want more, double the recipe.

Grilled Cheese

Grilled cheese is easy to make, but it's also incredibly easy to make poorly. I can't even count the number of times I failed at making grilled cheese sandwiches as a teenager. It sounds ridiculous now, but it's true. I'd always cook them over too high a heat, which meant I'd nearly burn my sandwiches before the cheese had begun to melt.

Now, I'm an old hand at it, and, like the soba noodle bowl on page 48, grilled cheese sandwiches make a super-satisfying dinner, especially after late work nights. After all, I always have cheese in the fridge, and, of course, once you know what you're doing, it's simple to throw together. (Even my husband can whip it up.)

As for the ingredients, the choice of bread and cheese is extremely important. Select bread that'll crisp up nicely on the outside, and choose cheese that melts beautifully. For the bread, I prefer wheat sourdough, and for the cheese, I rotate between Havarti, Taleggio, and fontina (and occasionally a little Brie, Gorgonzola, or blue cheese for flavor). My basic Grown-Up Grilled Cheese is great as it is, but the fillings in each variation make it sublime.

Grown-Up Grilled Cheese

YIELD: 2 SANDWICHES

. . . .

4 slices whole wheat sourdough bread
1 clove garlic
1 to 2 tablespoons (14 to 28 g) unsalted butter, softened
2 ounces (56 g) sliced Havarti cheese
2 ounces (56 g) sliced Taleggio cheese

Preheat a large skillet or griddle over medium-low heat. Take each slice of bread, cut the garlic in half, and rub the cut side over the bread. Spread the butter on each outer side of the bread.

Place one slice of bread, buttered side down, in the pan, then layer on 1 ounce (28 g) each Havarti and Taleggio cheese. Top with the remaining piece of bread, buttered side up. Cook for 6 to 7 minutes, flip, and cook for another 6 to 7 minutes, until each side is golden and the cheese has melted. Repeat with the remaining ingredients to make the second sandwich.

Spiced Eggplant Grilled Cheese

SPRING

Apricot and Three Cheese

YIELD: 2 SANDWICHES

. . . .

1 recipe Grown-Up Grilled Cheese (page 51)
2 just-ripe apricots, thinly sliced
¼ red onion, thinly sliced
2 teaspoons balsamic vinegar
1 teaspoon honey
½ ounce (14 g) Gorgonzola

Combine the apricots and onion in a bowl. Stir in the balsamic vinegar and honey and toss until the apricots are coated.

Make the Grown-Up Grilled Cheese as directed, substituting the Gorgonzola cheese for 1 ounce (28 g) of Havarti and layering in the red onion and apricot mixture when assembling the grilled cheese.

 For extra flavor, try roasting the honey-coated apricots and onion at 400°F (200°C, or gas mark 6) for 12 to 15 minutes before using.

 SUMMER

Spiced Eggplant

YIELD: 2 SANDWICHES

. . . .

1 recipe Grown-Up Grilled Cheese (page 51)
Four ¼-inch (6 mm) slices of eggplant
1 tablespoon (15 ml) olive oil
½ teaspoon cumin
¼ teaspoon smoked paprika
¼ teaspoon sea salt
¼ teaspoon black pepper

Light the grill. Toss the eggplant slices with the olive oil, cumin, smoked paprika, sea salt, and black pepper. Grill for 1 to 2 minutes, flip, and cook for another 1 to 2 minutes, until tender.

Make the Grown-Up Grilled Cheese as directed, layering the eggplant with the cheese when assembling the sandwich.

FALL

Spinach and Onion

YIELD: 2 SANDWICHES

. . . .

1 recipe Grown-Up Grilled Cheese (page 51)
½ tablespoon olive oil
½ small yellow onion, thinly sliced
¼ teaspoon sea salt
1 cup (40 g) baby spinach
2 ounces (56 g) whole-milk mozzarella cheese
2 to 3 teaspoons spicy brown mustard

Heat the olive oil in a skillet over medium-low heat. Add the onion and salt and cook until tender and starting to brown, 10 to 12 minutes. Stir the onions occasionally. If the onions are browning too quickly, reduce to the heat to low. Turn off the heat, add the spinach to the pan, cover, and let sit until the spinach is slightly wilted, 1 to 2 minutes. Rinse out the skillet and return to the stove.

Make the Grown-Up Grilled Cheese as directed, substituting the mozzarella cheese for the Taleggio. Layer in the spinach and spread the mustard on one side of each piece of bread when assembling the grilled cheese.

 WINTER

Butternut Squash and Hummus

YIELD: 2 SANDWICHES

. . . .

1 recipe Grown-Up Grilled Cheese (page 51)
8 slices butternut squash, each sliced into ¼-inch (6 mm) thick half moons
6 slices red onion, each sliced into ¼-inch (6 mm) thick half-moons
1 tablespoon (15 ml) olive oil
¼ teaspoon salt
⅛ teaspoon black pepper
2 ounces (54 g) fontina cheese
¼ cup (60 g) Traditional Hummus (page 84)

Preheat the oven to 400°F (200°C, or gas mark 6). Toss the butternut squash and onions with the olive oil, salt, and black pepper. Spread out on a baking tray and roast for 30 minutes, until tender.

Make the Grown-Up Grilled Cheese as directed, substituting the fontina cheese for the Taleggio. Layer the roasted butternut squash and onions on the grilled cheese when assembling and spread 2 tablespoons (30 g) of the hummus on the inside of each sandwich.

Panzanella Salad

When I make salads, I have a tendency to go overboard with the croutons. Way overboard. In fact, some of my salads involve more croutons than vegetables. So, when I first came across a salad with stale bread as its main ingredient, I was beyond excited—clearly, others shared my love of bread-laden salads!

Meet panzanella, an Italian salad with a fairly straightforward concept. Take a few chunks of stale bread, add fresh tomatoes, fresh basil, and a healthy drizzle of olive oil and balsamic vinegar, and you've got a meal. For my version, I create my own "stale" bread by making homemade croutons, and I serve it up with my favorite mustardy vinaigrette.

Don't let the long list of ingredients for panzanella salads deter you. You'll have most of the ingredients on hand in your fridge or pantry anyway, and this salad is such a fun way to use up bread that's on the stale side. Plus, it's quick to make—individual parts can be prepared ahead of time and assembled right before serving. And the dressing is so darn good that I often whip up extra to use on other salads throughout the week.

Pantry Panzanella

YIELD: 2 SERVINGS

Bread Cubes

2 cups (100 g) multigrain or sourdough
    cubed bread
1 tablespoon (15 ml) olive oil
¼ teaspoon sea salt
¼ teaspoon black pepper

Salad

2 to 3 cups (240 to 360 g) chunked
    heirloom tomatoes
1 medium cucumber, diced
½ medium red onion, diced
2 tablespoons (5 g) shredded basil, plus extra
    for garnish
3 cups (120 g) packed shredded lettuce

Dressing

2 tablespoons (30 ml) olive oil
1 tablespoon (15 ml) balsamic vinegar
1 teaspoon stone-ground mustard
¼ teaspoon salt
¼ teaspoon pepper
1 to 2 teaspoons honey

To make the bread cubes: Preheat the oven to 375°F (190°C, or gas mark 5). Toss together the cubed bread, olive oil, sea salt, and black pepper. Bake until crisp, 12 to 14 minutes. Remove from the oven and let cool slightly.

To make the salad: In a bowl, toss together the tomatoes, cucumber, red onion, and basil.

To make the dressing: In a separate bowl, whisk together all the dressing ingredients. Pour the dressing over the tomato mixture, then fold in the toasted bread.

Place the lettuce in a serving bowl and spoon the tomato mixture on top. Serve with a final sprinkle of shredded basil.

 To make the panzanella a little more filling, toss a few small balls of fresh mozzarella into the salad along with the vegetables.

SPRING

Peas, Spinach, and Fennel

YIELD: 2 SERVINGS

. . . .

Salad

1 cup (100 g) thinly sliced fennel
1 cup (130 g) shelled peas
1 cup (20 g) pea shoots
2 tablespoons (14 g) sunflower seeds
1 tablespoon (6 g) minced garlic scapes
3 cups (120 g) packed chopped spinach

Dressing

1 recipe Pantry Panzanella Dressing (page 54)
2 tablespoons (30 ml) lemon juice
½ teaspoon lemon zest
1 recipe Pantry Panzanella Bread Cubes (page 54)

To make the salad: Combine the fennel, peas, pea shoots, sunflower seeds, and garlic in a bowl.

To make the dressing: Whisk together the Panzanella Dressing, adding the lemon juice and zest in place of the balsamic vinegar. Pour the dressing over the fennel mixture and let sit while finishing the salad.

When ready to serve, fold the bread cubes into the fennel mixture and serve over spinach.

 SUMMER

Grilled Panzanella with Burst Tomatoes

YIELD: 2 SERVINGS

. . . .

1 recipe Pantry Panzanella (page 54)
¾ pound (340 g) cherry and/or grape tomatoes

Bread Cubes

2 or 3 slices sourdough bread
1 tablespoon (15 ml) olive oil
¼ teaspoon sea salt
¼ teaspoon black pepper

Light the grill. In a foil pouch, combine the cherry tomatoes and diced onion. Seal and place the pouch on the grill, cooking until the tomatoes burst, 5 to 7 minutes. Remove from the grill and let cool slightly.

To make the bread cubes: Brush the bread slices with olive oil and sprinkle with salt and pepper. Place on the grill and cook until toasted, flipping once during grilling. Remove and cut into cubes.

Assemble the salad as directed, using the grilled bread in place of the bread cubes and using the burst tomatoes instead of the fresh.

FALL

Roasted Beet and Apple

YIELD: 2 SERVINGS

. . . .

1 recipe Pantry Panzanella (page 54)
2 medium red beets
1 tablespoon (15 ml) olive oil
1 medium apple, peeled and cubed
3 tablespoons (22 g) pecans
2 tablespoons (30 ml) apple cider vinegar
1 tablespoon (15 ml) maple syrup
1 ounce (28 g) blue cheese

Preheat the oven to 425°F (220°C, or gas mark 7). Peel and cut the beets in half, then cut each half into 6 pieces. Toss with the olive oil in a roasting pan. Cover the pan with foil and fold one corner back to let steam escape. Roast for 40 to 50 minutes, until tender. Add to a bowl along with the apple and pecans.

Whisk together the dressing as directed, adding the apple cider vinegar in place of the balsamic vinegar and the maple syrup in place of the honey, then toss with the beet mixture and bread cubes. Assemble the salad as directed, serving the beet mixture over the lettuce and sprinkling with the blue cheese.

 WINTER

Roasted Butternut Squash with Cornbread

YIELD: 2 SERVINGS WITH LEFTOVER CORNBREAD

. . . .

Cornbread
½ cup (60 g) whole wheat pastry flour
½ cup (78 g) cornmeal
1 teaspoon baking powder
¼ teaspoon sea salt
2 large eggs
2 tablespoons (30 ml) maple syrup
¼ cup (60 ml) walnut oil or melted butter
½ cup (120 ml) milk

Butternut Squash
3 cups (420 g) ¼-inch (6 mm) cubed butternut squash
1 tablespoon (15 ml) olive oil
¼ teaspoon salt
½ teaspoon smoked paprika
¼ teaspoon garlic powder
1 tablespoon (15 ml) maple syrup

Salad
3 cups (120 g) loose-leaf lettuce
1 ounce (28 g) blue cheese
2 hard-boiled eggs
3 tablespoons (22 g) walnuts
1 recipe Pantry Panzanella Dressing (page 54)

To make the cornbread: Preheat the oven to 350°F (180°C, or gas mark 4). Grease an 8 by 8-inch (20 by 20 cm) baking pan or line with parchment paper.

In a bowl, combine the flour, cornmeal, baking powder, and salt. In a separate bowl, whisk together the eggs, maple syrup, oil, and milk. Pour the wet ingredients into the dry, and stir until well combined. Pour the cornbread batter into the prepared pan and bake for 25 to 30 minutes until firm when pressed and a knife comes out clean when inserted.

Increase the heat to 400°F (200°C, or gas mark 6).

Let the cornbread cool and cut into ¼-inch (6 mm) cubes. Measure out 2 cups (200 g) and save the rest for another use. Spread on a baking sheet and bake for 15 minutes, until the cornbread is dried out and crisp.

To make the squash: Toss the squash with the olive oil, salt, garlic powder, paprika and maple syrup. Spread in a thin layer in a roasting pan and bake for 25 to 30 minutes, until tender.

To make the salad: In a bowl, toss together the lettuce, cornbread, roasted butternut squash, blue cheese, hard-boiled eggs, and walnuts. Drizzle the dressing over the salad and toss until well coated.

Polenta

Every vegetarian cook should have a recipe for polenta in his or her toolbox. Why? It's just so versatile. (And so reassuring: when I'm in need of comfort food, I always turn to polenta.) Freshly cooked, it provides a lovely, creamy base for herbs, cheeses, vegetables, and even the occasional egg. Skip the prepackaged stuff and make it at home—it's not difficult. Cooking times vary, though. It can cook as quickly as 15 minutes, but you can also leave it to cook longer so that its flavors really develop. I often make slow-cooked polenta as a companion to roasted vegetables, adding a little extra protein by tossing a few beans on top.

Cooked, cooled polenta can also be cut into slices and then grilled, baked, or fried. You simply transfer the cooled polenta to a dish, pat it down, and leave to cool. Once cool, it can be cut into shapes and used as a companion for grilled or roasted vegetables, or it can even be deep-fried for a fun treat. Or, to recreate last night's creamy polenta, just add some extra milk to the leftovers, then reheat.

Creamy Polenta

YIELD: 4 SERVINGS

4 cups (960 ml) water
1 cup (180 g) polenta
½ teaspoon salt
2 tablespoons (28 g) unsalted butter
¼ cup (30 ml) whole milk
2 ounces (56 g) shredded cheese (optional)

Bring the water to a boil in a large pot over high heat. Add the polenta and salt, then reduce the heat to low. Cover, and let cook for 25 to 30 minutes, stirring every 5 minutes. Taste and adjust the salt as desired.

Once the polenta is cooked, remove from the heat and stir in the butter, milk, and cheese. Serve with your favorite vegetables, beans, and herbs.

 Cook the polenta over very low heat. It's best to use the lowest setting on your stove top. If your range has the option, place the pot on the burner marked for simmering. If you think your stove top heats up more quickly, check and stir the polenta more frequently.

Goat Cheese Polenta with Crispy Beets

 SPRING

Goat Cheese Polenta with Crispy Beets

YIELD: 4 SERVINGS

. . . .

1 recipe Creamy Polenta (page 57)
2 ounces (56 g) soft goat cheese, divided
2 medium red or chioggia beets
1 tablespoon (15 ml) olive oil
¼ teaspoon sea salt
¼ teaspoon black pepper
2 to 3 tablespoons (14 to 22 g) roasted sunflower seeds

Make the polenta as directed, using 1½ ounces (42 g) of the goat cheese in the final step.

Preheat the oven to 325°F (170°C, or gas mark 3). Cover baking sheets with parchment paper. Wash and peel the beets. Using a mandolin or sharp knife, slice the beets as thinly as possible. Toss them with the olive oil, sea salt, and black pepper. Place in a single layer on the baking sheets. Roast for 15 to 20 minutes, until the beets are beginning to crisp. Remove from the oven and let cool to crisp further.

Sprinkle the polenta with the crispy beets, the remaining goat cheese, and the sunflower seeds right before serving.

 Check the beets frequently while roasting, and remove any pieces that crisp faster than the rest so they don't burn.

 SUMMER

Grilled Polenta with Chick-peas and Ginger Chutney

YIELD: 16 POLENTA SQUARES

. . . .

1 recipe Creamy Polenta (page 57)
1 cup (260 g) chickpeas
2 tablespoons (30 ml) olive oil, divided
1 tablespoon (15 ml) lemon juice
1 teaspoon each lemon zest and turmeric
¼ teaspoon each chili powder and sea salt
½ teaspoon black pepper, divided
1 recipe Ginger Chutney (page 106)
Chopped cilantro, for serving
Freshly squeezed lemon juice, for serving

Make the polenta as directed but leave out the milk. Pat the polenta into a lightly greased 8 by 8-inch (20 by 20 cm) pan and allow to cool. Once cool, slice into 2-inch (5 cm) squares and carefully remove from the pan.

Preheat the grill. Combine the chickpeas, 1 tablespoon (15 ml) of the olive oil, lemon juice and zest, turmeric, chili powder, salt, and ¼ teaspoon of the pepper in a foil package and place on the grill. Cook for 5 to 6 minutes. Brush the polenta with the remaining olive oil and sprinkle with the remaining black pepper. Using a grill pan, grill the polenta until lightly charred, 3 to 4 minutes on each side.

Remove the chickpeas from the grill and stir into the chutney. Spoon the chickpea mixture over the grilled polenta and finish with a sprinkle of cilantro and a squeeze of lemon juice.

FALL

Sweet Potato-Swirled Polenta with Poached Egg

YIELD: 4 SERVINGS

. . . .

1 recipe Creamy Polenta (page 57)
1 medium sweet potato
¼ cup (60 ml) vegetable broth
2 teaspoons fresh rosemary, minced
¼ teaspoon black pepper
¼ teaspoon sea salt
Olive oil, for topping
4 poached eggs

Bring a pot of water to a boil with a pinch of salt. Peel the sweet potato, cut into ½-inch (1.3 cm) cubes, and boil until tender, 5 to 8 minutes. Drain the sweet potatoes and place in a food processor with the vegetable broth, rosemary, black pepper, and salt. Pulse until smooth.

Swirl the sweet potato purée into the polenta and top each serving with a drizzle of olive oil and a poached egg.

 WINTER

Caramelized Cauliflower Polenta

YIELD: 4 SERVINGS

. . . .

1 recipe Creamy Polenta (page 57)
5 cups (350 g) bite-size cauliflower florets
¼ cup (30 g) red curry paste
2 tablespoons (30 ml) freshly squeezed lime juice
1 tablespoon (15 ml) olive oil
Chopped cilantro, for serving
Freshly squeezed lime juice, for serving

Preheat the oven to 400°F (200°C, or gas mark 6). In a bowl, toss the cauliflower florets with the curry paste, lime juice, and olive oil. Spread in an even layer in a roasting pan. Bake until the cauliflower is tender and browning, 30 to 35 minutes.

Make the polenta as directed and top with the roasted cauliflower. Serve with a sprinkle of cilantro and a squeeze of fresh lime juice.

 Curry paste can be found in most stores in the ethnic food aisle.

Quesadillas

In our marriage, I am the cook and my husband is not. We made this arrangement very early on and I was okay with that. One day, one of our close friends—who also happens to be a chef—was visiting. When I came home from work, I was surprised to find quesadillas made with homemade tortillas waiting for me! I looked at our friend, who gleefully pointed at my husband: he'd done all the work. Suffice it to say that these homemade quesadillas hold a pretty special place in my heart.

Making tortillas might seem a bit tedious, but they make a huge difference to your meal. Using whole wheat and all-purpose flours keeps the tortillas soft and pliable, but you can use all whole wheat pastry flour, if you want. When I make this recipe, I often double it and freeze the extra. Having ready-to-use tortillas at my fingertips makes for an extremely quick meal. They can also be used as sandwich wraps, or if you make the tortillas a bit smaller, as taco or fajita shells.

As for fillings, a cheese quesadilla, if you ask me, requires little more than, say, a few tomatoes and onions for flavor. I try not to overload quesadillas, but I like to fill them so that they still feel like substantial meals. There's really no wrong way here, so fill to your heart's content.

Quesadillas with Wheat Tortillas

YIELD: 4 QUESADILLAS

. . . .

Wheat Tortillas
1 cup (120 g) whole wheat pastry flour
1 cup (120 g) unbleached all-purpose flour
½ teaspoon salt
½ teaspoon baking powder
¼ cup (60 ml) olive oil
½ cup (120 ml) warm water

Filling
Olive oil, for brushing
1 clove garlic, sliced in half
4 to 5 ounces (112 to 140 g) shredded
    Cheddar cheese
2 tablespoons (2 g) minced cilantro

To make the wheat tortillas: Combine the flours, salt, and baking powder in a bowl. Add the olive oil and, using your hands, rub it into the flour to form a shaggy mixture. Stir in the water and form a ball. Cover and let rest for 20 minutes.

Preheat a large skillet or griddle over medium-low heat. Divide the dough into 4 balls and, on a lightly floured surface, roll one ball into a rough, 10-inch (25 cm) circle. Place in the skillet and cook on each side for 1 to 2 minutes, until lightly browned and small air pockets form. Cover with a damp towel and continue with the remaining dough.

To make the filling: Heat a griddle to medium-low. Brush the outer sides of two tortillas with olive oil and rub with the halved garlic. Place one tortilla on the griddle and sprinkle with half the cheese. Cover with the second tortilla and cook for 2 to 3 minutes. Carefully flip and cook for another 3 to 4 minutes. Repeat with the remaining tortillas and filling. Slice in half and serve.

 Store leftover tortillas in an airtight bag in the refrigerator for 2 to 3 days, or freeze for extended storage.

< Mashed Avocado and Cilantro Quesadilla

SPRING

Scallion and Spinach

YIELD: 4 QUESADILLAS

. . . .

1 recipe Wheat Tortillas (page 61)
¼ cup (24 g) diced scallion
2 cups (80 g) packed shredded spinach
1 teaspoon lime juice
⅛ teaspoon red pepper flakes
4 ounces (112 g) queso quesadilla cheese

Make the wheat tortillas as directed. Combine the diced
scallion, shredded spinach, lime juice, and red pepper flakes in
a bowl. Assemble the quesadillas using half the *queso* cheese
and half the spinach mixture for each quesadilla.

 SUMMER

Adobo Grilled Eggplant

YIELD: 4 QUESADILLAS

. . . .

Adobo Seasoning
2 tablespoons (10 g) smoked paprika
1 tablespoon (5 g) onion powder
1 tablespoon (2 g) dried Mexican oregano
2 teaspoons garlic powder
2 teaspoons chipotle powder
1½ teaspoons black pepper
1½ teaspoons sea salt
1 teaspoon cumin powder
2 tablespoons (30 g) turbinado or brown sugar

Eggplant
Eight ¼-inch (6 mm) slices eggplant
2 tablespoons (30 ml) olive oil
4 ounces (112 g) Taleggio cheese
1 recipe Wheat Tortillas (page 61)

To make the seasoning: In a small bowl, whisk together all the
seasoning ingredients. Set aside 2 tablespoons (20 g) and store
the remainder for future use.

To make the eggplant: Light a grill to medium heat. In a large
bowl, combine the eggplant slices with the olive oil and adobo
seasoning, tossing until the eggplant is well coated. Grill for 2
to 3 minutes on each side, just until starting to brown. Remove
the eggplant, let cool slightly, and cut into smaller pieces.

Make the quesadillas as directed, filling the tortillas with the
Taleggio cheese and grilled eggplant.

FALL

Mashed Avocado and Cilantro

YIELD: 4 QUESADILLAS

. . . .

1 recipe Wheat Tortillas (page 61)
2 ripe avocados
¼ cup (4 g) minced cilantro
2 tablespoons (30 ml) lime juice
⅛ teaspoon sea salt
4 ounces (112 g) queso quesadilla cheese

Cut each avocado in half and scoop out the flesh into a small bowl. Add the cilantro, lime juice, and salt. Mash the avocado with the back of a fork, incorporating the lime juice and cilantro as you mash.

Make the quesadillas as directed, spreading the mashed avocado onto each quesadilla and layering the cheese on top before cooking.

 For a bit of a kick, add 1 tablespoon (9 g) minced jalapeño to the filling.

 WINTER

Spicy Brussels Sprouts

YIELD: 4 QUESADILLAS

. . . .

1 recipe Wheat Tortillas (page 61)
1 tablespoon (15 ml) olive oil
1 shallot, finely chopped
½ pound (230 g) Brussels sprouts, shredded
¼ teaspoon sea salt
½ teaspoon red pepper flakes
2 tablespoons (30 ml) water
4 to 5 ounces (112 to 140 g) shredded Cheddar cheese

Heat the olive oil in a skillet over medium heat. Add the shallot and cook for 2 to 3 minutes. Stir in the shredded Brussels sprouts, salt, red pepper flakes, and water. Cook, stirring occasionally, until the sprouts are tender, 4 to 5 minutes.

Make the quesadillas as directed, filling with the cooked Brussels sprouts and cheese from the original recipe.

Egg Skillet

It doesn't take more than a quick glance at the archives of my blog to figure out that I love three things in particular: tacos, any type of dish involving noodles, and egg skillets. My relationship with egg skillets began when I happened upon a well-seasoned, 8-inch (20 cm) cast-iron skillet in an antique shop a few years back. One of the first recipes I made with it incorporated leftover cooked grains with a random assortment of vegetables and two eggs cracked over the top. Ever since then, the egg skillet has become an old reliable, especially when I'm just cooking for myself.

When I lived alone, this meal happened—in many different forms—nearly every day of the week. It's simple, it lets you use whatever kind of produce you have on hand, it always leaves you full and satisfied, and it's delicious. The bottom of the vegetables crisp and caramelize as the eggs cook, creating a nice balance of textures.

My egg skillets typically make single servings, but the recipe can easily be doubled and made in a 12-inch (30 cm) skillet to serve two or three. Just keep a close eye on the eggs and make sure the heat stays low; otherwise, the vegetables and grains will burn. If you want to skip the cheese, go ahead; more often than not I forget about it myself until I'm halfway through eating. It's totally optional, but it does add a nice finishing touch to the skillet.

Easy Egg Skillet

YIELD: 1 OR 2 SERVINGS

. . . .

1 tablespoon (15 ml) olive oil
¼ cup (35 g) diced red onion
2 cups (320 g) chopped assorted vegetables
¼ teaspoon sea salt
¼ teaspoon black pepper
½ cup (80 g) cooked grains (optional)
2 large eggs
½ ounce (14 g) grated cheese (optional)

Heat the olive oil over medium-low heat in an 8-inch (20 cm) cast-iron or nonstick skillet. Add the diced onion and cook until translucent and fragrant, 6 to 7 minutes. Stir in the vegetables, and cook until tender (time will vary based on the vegetable).

Add the salt, pepper, and grains, stirring until well combined. Form a well in the center of the mixture and crack in the eggs. Reduce the heat to the lowest setting, cover, and cook until the egg whites are set and the egg yolk is at the desired firmness, 8 to 10 minutes for over-easy and 12 to 14 minutes for over-hard. Remove from the heat and serve with a sprinkle of cheese.

Cauliflower and Goat Cheese Egg Skillet >

SPRING

Bok Choy, Sesame, and Rice

YIELD: 1 OR 2 SERVINGS

. . . .

1 recipe Easy Egg Skillet (page 64)
½ bunch (55 g) scallions
2 cups (80 g) shredded bok choy leaves, lightly packed
½ cup (76 g) cooked barley
1 tablespoon (7 g) toasted sesame seeds
Soy or tamari sauce, for serving

Make the egg skillet as directed, using scallions in place of onions and cooking the bok choy until just wilted. Serve the skillet with the toasted sesame seeds and a drizzle of soy sauce.

 SUMMER

Grilled Sweet Corn

YIELD: 1 OR 2 SERVINGS

. . . .

1 recipe Easy Egg Skillet (page 64)
1 cup (120 g) sweet corn kernels
¼ teaspoon chipotle powder
½ cup (80 g) cooked brown rice
2 tablespoons (2 g) minced cilantro, plus more for serving
½ ounce (14 g) crumbled cotija cheese
Lime wedges, for serving

Make the egg skillet as directed, stirring in the corn and chipotle powder after the onions have been added; cook until the corn is lightly charred, 6 to 7 minutes. Add the brown rice and cilantro, and continue as directed. Serve with an extra sprinkle of cilantro and the crumbled cheese. Garnish with a lime wedge.

 FALL

Cauliflower and Goat Cheese

YIELD: 1 OR 2 SERVINGS

. . . .

1 recipe Easy Egg Skillet (page 64)
¼ cup (35 g) diced yellow onion
1½ cups (160 g) cauliflower pieces
½ cup (80 g) cooked brown rice
½ ounce (14 g) goat cheese
Parsley, for serving

Make the egg skillet as directed, substituting the yellow onion for the red and adding the cauliflower after the onions have softened; cook until tender, 7 to 8 minutes. Stir in the brown rice and continue as directed. Serve with a sprinkle of goat cheese and parsley.

 WINTER

Mushroom and Garlic

YIELD: 1 OR 2 SERVINGS

. . . .

1 recipe Easy Egg Skillet (page 64)
1 clove garlic, minced
2 cups (140 g) sliced cremini mushrooms
1 cup (140 g) cooked quinoa
1 teaspoon fresh thyme

Make the egg skillet as directed, using the garlic in place of the onions. Cook the garlic for 1 minute, add the mushrooms and cook for another 4 to 5 minutes, just until tender. Add the quinoa and thyme, and continue as directed.

Fried Rice Bowl

By now you've probably noticed that I'm a lover of leftovers. Whether they're enough for full meals or consist of nothing more than a handful or two of cooked grains, I work leftovers into just about every meal I make. When I had to commute for work, I'd spend big chunks of my weekends cooking up large batches of beans and grains—especially rice—to use throughout the week. Dinners were all about black-bean-and-rice bowls, or large batches of fried rice that I could eat for lunch the next day.

The premise of fried rice is pretty simple: take leftover cooked rice and lightly fry it with vegetables and eggs. I think the fried rice you get in restaurants is a bit on the greasy side, so my recipe cuts back drastically on the oil, but it doesn't skimp on taste.

What's more, this fried rice is yet another great way to use up just about any vegetables that may be past their prime. Just finely dice them, add them to the pan, and cook them before adding the rice. And speaking of rice, I typically cook with short-grain rice because I prefer the texture. That said, either short- or long-grain rice will work well.

Healthier Fried Rice Bowl

YIELD: 2 SERVINGS

. . . .

1 tablespoon (15 ml) olive oil
1 clove garlic, minced
2 cups (320 g) cooked brown rice
3 tablespoons (45 ml) soy sauce
1 tablespoon (15 ml) rice wine vinegar
2 large eggs
2 tablespoons (14 g) sesame seeds
½ teaspoon black pepper

Heat the olive oil over low heat in a large skillet. Add the minced garlic and cook for 1 minute. Stir in the brown rice, soy sauce, and vinegar, and cook for 2 to 3 more minutes. Create a well in the center and crack the eggs. Let them set most of the way, 3 to 4 minutes, before stirring them into the rice mixture. Stir in the sesame seeds and black pepper. Serve hot.

SPRING

Roasted Snow Peas and Carrot

YIELD: 2 SERVINGS

. . . .

1 recipe Healthier Fried Rice Bowl (page 67)
4 ounces (112 g) snow peas, roughly chopped
½ cup (70 g) ¼-inch (6 mm) sliced carrot
½ tablespoon (7.5 ml) olive oil
1 tablespoon (8 g) sesame seeds

Preheat the oven to 400°F (200°C, or gas mark 6). Toss the snow peas and carrots together with the olive oil and sesame seeds. Spread on a baking sheet and roast for 25 to 30 minutes, until the snow peas start to blister.

Make the rice bowl as directed, adding the snow pea mixture in with the rice.

 SUMMER

Spicy Green Bean

YIELD: 2 SERVINGS

. . . .

1 recipe Healthier Fried Rice Bowl (page 67)
8 ounces (230 g) fresh green beans
2 tablespoons (30 ml) sriracha

Bring a pot of water to a boil. Add the green beans and blanch for 3 minutes. Drain and set aside. Once slightly cool, cut into ½-inch (1.3 cm) pieces.

Make the rice bowl as directed, adding the green beans and sriracha in with the garlic.

 FALL

Bean Sprouts and Kale

YIELD: 2 SERVINGS

. . . .

1 recipe Healthier Fried Rice Bowl (page 67)
2 cups (80 g) shredded dinosaur kale
½ cup (30 g) bean sprouts

Make the rice bowl as directed, adding the kale along with the brown rice. Before serving, top with the bean sprouts.

 WINTER

Three Onion

YIELD: 2 SERVINGS

. . . .

1 recipe Healthier Fried Rice Bowl (page 67)
½ tablespoon (7 ml) olive oil
1 shallot, diced
½ cup (70 g) diced red onion
½ cup (70 g) diced white onion

Heat the olive oil in a skillet over low heat. Add the diced shallot and onions and cook for 10 to 12 minutes, stirring occasionally, until tender. Make the rice bowl as directed, using the onion mixture in place of the garlic.

< *Spicy Green Bean Rice Bowl*

Loaded Potatoes

As the natural foods movement grows, so, it seems, do popular viewpoints on certain foods. Kale, once relegated to the shelves of food co-ops, is now sold in abundance at supermarket chains. Quinoa, once a word hardly anyone knew how to pronounce, is now a celebrated grain that gets top billing on restaurant menus. And then you have those items that get the opposite treatment—like the humble potato. Even though potatoes don't pack the same punch of flavor (or nutrients) as some other ingredients, they make great bases for recipes.

I'm a big fan of potatoes, and the truth is, I eat just as many regular potatoes as I do sweet potatoes. I love making homemade French fries to accompany vegetable burgers, adding cubed potatoes to stews, and, best of all, using them as a foundation for an easy meal. Though the russet potato may not be quite as rich in nutrients as the sweet potato, spuds are still a healthy choice, and can feature in plenty of your meals.

The first time I had a loaded potato, it was smothered with vegetarian chili and cheese. (Drool.) And it wasn't just delicious: it was also a healthy, filling meal. Then I expanded my repertoire of toppings, and now these loaded potatoes make regular appearances on the menu in our house. I use russet potatoes and sweet potatoes interchangeably, based on what I have on hand. Plus, the untopped potato can also make a nice base for the lentil stew on page 76.

Basic Loaded Potatoes

YIELD: 2 TO 4 SERVINGS

. . . .

2 medium russet potatoes or sweet potatoes
1 tablespoon (15 ml) olive oil
2 tablespoons (30 ml) heavy cream
1 tablespoon (14 g) unsalted butter, melted
¼ teaspoon sea salt
¼ teaspoon black pepper

Preheat the oven to 425°F (220°C, or gas mark 7). Scrub the potatoes, pierce a few times with a fork, and rub with olive oil. Place in a roasting pan and bake until soft and a knife can be inserted with ease, 45 to 55 minutes. Remove from the oven and carefully slice in half. Scoop out the insides and mix with the heavy cream, butter, salt, and pepper. Fill the potato skins with the potato mixture and top with your favorite topping.

SPRING

Buttered White Bean and Gremolata

YIELD: 2 TO 4 SERVINGS

. . . .

1 recipe Basic Loaded Potatoes (page 70)
2 tablespoons (28 g) unsalted butter
1 cup (260 g) cooked cannellini beans (drained and rinsed if using canned)
¼ teaspoon sea salt
¼ teaspoon black pepper
1 clove garlic, minced
2 teaspoons lemon zest
¼ cup (15 g) minced parsley

Prepare the Basic Loaded Potatoes as directed.

Melt the butter in a skillet over low heat. Add the beans, salt, and pepper and cook until warm, 3 to 4 minutes. In a small bowl, combine the minced garlic, lemon zest, and parsley.

Divide the bean mixture among the potatoes halves and finish with a sprinkle of the garlic mixture.

 Gremolata is a garnish made with minced parsley, lemon peel, and garlic.

 SUMMER

Grilled Vegetable with Cheese and Hummus

YIELD: 2 TO 4 SERVINGS

. . . .

1 recipe Basic Loaded Potatoes (page 70)
1 small zucchini
¼ red onion
½ red pepper
1 tablespoon (15 ml) olive oil
1 teaspoon smoked paprika
½ teaspoon garlic powder
½ teaspoon sea salt
1 ounce (28 g) feta cheese
¼ cup (60 g) Traditional Hummus (page 84)

Prepare the Basic Loaded Potatoes as directed.

Light a grill and prepare the vegetables by cutting the zucchini and onion into ¼-inch (6 mm) thick slices and the red pepper into quarters. Brush with the olive oil and sprinkle with the smoked paprika, garlic powder, and sea salt. Grill, flipping halfway through, until the vegetables are starting to char, 3 to 5 minutes. Remove from the heat and dice.

Divide the vegetable mixture among the potato halves, sprinkle with the feta, and serve with a dollop of hummus.

FALL

Curried Cauliflower with Yogurt

YIELD: 2 WHOLE POTATOES OR 4 HALVES

. . . .

1 recipe Basic Loaded Potatoes (page 70)
1 tablespoon (15 ml) olive oil
2 cloves garlic, minced
½ cup (120 ml) full-fat coconut milk
¾ to 1 cup (180 to 240 ml) low-sodium vegetable broth
½ teaspoon sea salt
1 tablespoon (6 g) curry powder
3 cups (240 g) cauliflower pieces
½ cup (130 g) chickpeas
Chopped cilantro, for serving
Plain whole-milk Greek-style yogurt, for serving

Prepare the Basic Loaded Potatoes as directed.

In a large skillet, heat the olive oil over medium-low heat and cook the garlic for 1 minute. Whisk in the coconut milk, broth, salt, and curry powder. Add the cauliflower and chickpeas. Bring to a boil, reduce to a simmer, cover, and let cook until the cauliflower is tender and the sauce has reduced down slightly, 20 to 22 minutes.

Divide the mixture among the potato halves, sprinkle with cilantro, and top with a spoonful of Greek yogurt.

 WINTER

Creamy Millet with Kale

YIELD: 2 TO 4 SERVINGS

. . . .

1 recipe Basic Loaded Potatoes (page 70)
1 tablespoon (15 ml) olive oil
1 clove garlic, minced
½ cup (76 g) uncooked millet
1½ cups (360 ml) water
½ teaspoon sea salt
¼ teaspoon black pepper
1 cup (70 g) shredded dinosaur kale, packed
3 tablespoons (18 g) mascarpone cheese
⅓ cup (80 ml) whole milk

Make the Basic Loaded Potatoes as directed.

In a pot, heat the olive oil over medium-low heat. Add the minced garlic and cook for 1 to 2 minutes. Stir in the millet and cook for another minute. Next, add the water, salt, and black pepper. Bring to a boil, reduce to a simmer, and cook the millet for 22 to 24 minutes, until the water is mostly absorbed. Remove from the heat, stir in the shredded kale, cover, and let sit until the remaining water has been absorbed and the kale is wilted.

When ready to serve, stir in the mascarpone cheese and milk. Spoon over the prepared potatoes.

Grain Salad

On one of our very first dates, my husband ordered a huge salad for dinner. I remember being surprised because, until then, the men I'd met approached salads as appetizers only. Not my husband, though! To this day, he'd jump at the chance to have a salad as a meal.

You can imagine, then, how seriously we take salads at our house. My husband doesn't really follow a recipe—he tends to throw whatever's hiding in the refrigerator and cupboards into his salads. Mine are a little more structured, and they go something like this: Start with a handful of greens, and top them with fresh, roasted, or grilled vegetables; a scoop of cooked grains; and a sprinkle of nuts, seeds, and cheese; follow with some kind of protein (typically legumes or hard-boiled eggs); drizzle with a simple homemade vinaigrette. It's hard to go wrong—really!—but the recipes that follow will give you a little inspiration to get you started.

One caveat, though: great salads need very crisp, fresh greens. If you eat salads as often as I do, invest in a salad spinner so that you can dry your washed greens thoroughly. And be sure to keep an assortment of nuts and seeds (and even dried fruit!) in the cupboard so you have plenty of fun toppings at your fingertips. And, as always, experiment with these recipes as much as you like.

Grilled Greens and Millet Salad

Perfect Grain Salad

YIELD: 2 SERVINGS

. . . .

Salad

3 cups (120 g) packed greens, such as lettuce, spinach, or kale
2 cups (320 g) diced assorted vegetables
1 cup (160 g) cooked grains, cooled
¼ cup (25 g) nuts, in pieces
1 ounce (28 g) crumbled or shredded cheese
2 hard-boiled eggs, sliced

Dressing

3 tablespoons (45 ml) olive oil
2 tablespoons (30 ml) champagne vinegar
2 teaspoons honey
¼ teaspoon sea salt
¼ teaspoon black pepper

To make the salad: Wash and dry the greens, then place in a large bowl. Top with the vegetables, grains, nuts, and cheese. Toss until well combined.

To make the dressing: In a small bowl, whisk together the olive oil, vinegar, honey, salt, and pepper. Taste and adjust the flavors as desired. Pour over the greens and toss again until the greens are coated. Divide the salad among 2 bowls and top with the sliced egg.

SPRING

Fava Bean and Quinoa

YIELD: 2 SERVINGS

. . . .

1½ cups (270 g) fava beans, removed from pods
1 tablespoon (14 g) unsalted butter, melted
½ teaspoon fresh minced thyme
½ teaspoon fresh minced rosemary
3 cups (120 g) packed spinach
1 cup (140 g) cooked quinoa
2 tablespoons (32 g) toasted pine nuts
1 ounce (28 g) crumbled feta cheese
1 recipe Perfect Grain Salad Dressing (page 73)
2 hard-boiled eggs, sliced

Bring a large pot of water to a boil. Add the fava beans to the water, boil for 2 minutes, and transfer to an ice bath. Remove the outer skin from the fava beans, then toss them with the melted butter and fresh herbs.

Wash and dry the spinach, then place in a large bowl. Top with the fava beans, cooked quinoa, pine nuts, and feta. Toss until well combined.

Pour the dressing over the salad and toss again until the spinach is coated. Divide the salad among 2 bowls and top with the sliced egg.

 SUMMER

Grilled Greens and Millet

YIELD: 2 SERVINGS

. . . .

1 small head romaine lettuce
1 tablespoon (15 ml) olive oil
¼ teaspoon sea salt
1 cup (140 g) cherry tomatoes, sliced in half
½ cup (70 g) cubed cucumber
¼ cup (35 g) diced red onion
1 cup (152 g) cooked millet
1 ounce (28 g) goat cheese
2 tablespoons (5 g) minced fresh basil
1 recipe Perfect Grain Salad Dressing (page 73)
2 teaspoons brown mustard

Light a grill to medium-low heat. Slice the lettuce head in half lengthwise, and rub each half with olive oil and sprinkle with salt. Place cut side down on the grill and cook until the lettuce starts to wilt and is slightly charred, 2 to 3 minutes on each side.

In a large bowl, toss together the tomatoes, cucumber, red onion, millet, goat cheese, and basil. In a separate bowl, prepare the Perfect Grain Salad Dressing as directed, adding in the brown mustard. Pour the dressing over the millet mixture and stir until combined. Chop the grilled lettuce and fold into the vegetable-millet mixture.

Chili Sweet Potato and Kamut

YIELD: 2 SERVINGS

. . . .

Salad

1 medium sweet potato
1 tablespoon (15 ml) olive oil
1 teaspoon smoked paprika
¼ teaspoon chili powder
¼ teaspoon salt
¼ teaspoon garlic powder
3 cups (120 g) packed spinach
1 cup (76 g) cooked Kamut
¼ cup (25 g) roasted pumpkin seeds
3 tablespoons (3 g) minced cilantro
2 hard-boiled eggs, sliced

Dressing

1 tablespoon (15 ml) olive oil
1 tablespoon (15 ml) lime juice
2 teaspoons honey
¼ teaspoon salt
¼ teaspoon pepper

To make the salad: Preheat the oven to 400°F (200°C, or gas mark 6). Peel and cut the sweet potato into ¼-inch (6 mm) cubes. Toss the sweet potato cubes with the olive oil, smoked paprika, chili powder, salt, and garlic powder. Spread in a thin layer in a roasting pan and bake until tender, 20 to 25 minutes. Remove from the oven and let cool slightly. In a bowl, toss together the spinach, Kamut, pumpkin seeds, cilantro, and roasted sweet potatoes.

To make the dressing: Whisk together the ingredients for the dressing, pour over the salad, and toss until well coated. Serve with the hard-boiled egg slices.

Collards and Barley

YIELD: 2 SERVINGS

. . . .

2 cups (80 g) shredded collard greens
1 teaspoon lemon juice
1 cup (76 g) cooked barley, still slightly warm
2 tablespoons (14 g) sesame seeds
1 recipe Perfect Grain Salad Dressing (page 73)
1 teaspoon minced ginger
2 tablespoons (30 ml) soy sauce

Combine the collards with lemon juice, cooked barley, and sesame seeds. Allow to sit for 5 to 10 minutes to soften the collards. In a separate bowl, prepare the Perfect Grain Salad Dressing as directed, adding the minced ginger and using soy sauce in place of the vinegar. Pour over the salad and toss until well combined.

Lentil Stew

A few pages back, I made a bold claim: "If you have beans, you have a meal." I stand by it—and it's a maxim that applies to lentils, too. That's because dried lentils can be transformed into a meal in hardly any time at all. They absorb the flavors of whatever dish you're cooking, and they can easily be cooked to different consistencies to suit individual meals. Thanks to their ability to melt seamlessly into a dish, I keep red lentils on hand for curries and stews such as this one. Or, if I'm looking for a bit more texture and want the lentils to hold their shape, I choose green or brown lentils. And finally, if I want a meal in which lentils take a starring role, I grab Puy or black lentils.

Those are just loose guidelines, though. When I'm whipping up this stew, I use whatever type of lentil I have on hand, plus any vegetables that take my fancy. It also makes a wonderful freezer meal: just make an extra-large batch, divide it into individual freezer-safe containers, then pull out a batch whenever you need a lunch or dinner that's both quick and extremely filling.

Only the spring variation calls for cooked grains, but the truth is, I serve this lentil stew over cooked grains most of the time (though you can devour it on its own, of course). Also, I usually have a jar or two of strained tomatoes at the ready, but if you have fresh tomatoes on hand, use them: cook down slightly, purée, and use the purée in place of the strained tomatoes.

Seasonal Lentil Stew

YIELD: 3 TO 4 SERVINGS

1 tablespoon (15 ml) olive oil
½ medium red onion, diced
4 to 5 cups (960 to 1200 ml) vegetable broth
1 cup (168 g) red lentils
1 cup (240 ml) strained tomatoes
½ teaspoon salt
½ teaspoon black pepper
2 teaspoons oregano
1 tablespoon (2 g) fresh minced basil

In a skillet, heat the oil over low heat, then sweat the onions until translucent and fragrant, 7 to 8 minutes. Stir in all the remaining ingredients except the basil. Bring to a boil, reduce to a simmer, and let cook until the lentils are tender, 20 to 25 minutes. Stir in the basil, taste, and adjust the seasoning as desired.

Chard Over Garlic Rice Lentil Stew

SPRING

Chard Over Garlic Rice

YIELD: 3 TO 4 SERVINGS

. . . .

1 recipe Seasonal Lentil Stew (page 76)
1 cup (168 g) green lentils
2 cups (80 g) shredded and packed Swiss chard

Garlic Rice
1 tablespoon (15 ml) olive oil
1 clove garlic, minced
1 cup (180 g) long-grain brown rice
2 cups (480 ml) water

Make the stew as directed, substituting the green lentils for the red lentils. Once the lentils are tender, 25 to 30 minutes, add the Swiss chard and cook until wilted.

To make the rice: Heat the olive oil over medium-low heat in a medium saucepan. Add the garlic and cook for 1 minute. Stir in the rice, and toast for 1 minute more. Pour in the water, bring to a boil, reduce to a simmer, cover, and cook for 35 to 45 minutes, until the rice has absorbed all the water and is tender. Divide the rice among bowls and ladle the stew over.

 SUMMER

Roasted Red Pepper

YIELD: 3 TO 4 SERVINGS

. . . .

1 recipe Seasonal Lentil Stew (page 76)
2 red bell peppers
¼ cup (4 g) minced cilantro
2 teaspoons smoked paprika

Place the oven rack close to the top of the oven, turn on the broiler, place the red peppers under the flame, and cook, watching closely and rotating every 30 to 60 seconds, until the peppers are charred. Remove from the oven and let cool slightly. Remove the skin, core, and seeds, and dice the pepper.

Make the stew as directed, using the diced red pepper in place of the tomatoes, the cilantro in place of the basil, and adding the smoked paprika.

 FALL

Chipotle Butternut Squash

YIELD: 3 TO 4 SERVINGS

. . . .

1 recipe Seasonal Lentil Stew (page 76)
2 cups (280 g) ¼-inch (6 mm) cubed butternut squash
2 teaspoons chipotle powder
1 teaspoon smoked paprika

Prepare the stew as directed, leaving out the basil and adding in the cubed squash, chipotle powder, and smoked paprika with the vegetable broth. Adjust the cooking time until the squash is tender, 25 to 30 minutes.

 WINTER

Roasted Root Vegetable

YIELD: 3 TO 4 SERVINGS

. . . .

1 recipe Seasonal Lentil Stew (page 76)
1 cup (140 g) cubed parsnip
1 cup (140 g) cubed rutabaga
2 teaspoons minced fresh rosemary
2 teaspoons minced fresh oregano
2 teaspoons minced fresh sage

Prepare the stew as directed, leaving out the basil and adding in the cubed root vegetables and the minced rosemary, oregano, and sage.

4

Appetizers/Small Plates

Whenever my husband and I go out to dinner, we always have a tough time deciding what we're going to settle on for an appetizer. Our choices usually depend on our mood, but two general rules hold true: we're always up for a plate of hummus, or anything involving cheese. Occasionally, if we can't reach a compromise, we'll order two instead of one. (Although that's dangerous: both of us are notorious for filling up on appetizers, and having to take our main meal home!)

If I'm *really* stuck and can't decide what to have, I treat appetizers like tapas, and order a couple of items from the appetizer list for my main meal. Not only are the portion sizes more manageable, I'm also always intrigued at some of the bolder flavor combinations offered in the appetizers, such as smoky chipotle tacos or a curry-laced pastry.

That's why the real title for this chapter should be "Recipes People Would Classify as an Appetizer, but I Eat as a Meal." And you could easily do the same! You'll find that some of the appetizers in this chapter are easily made in 5 minutes, like the hummus on page 84, while others are more time-consuming (but in my mind, well worth it), such as the potstickers on page 80. Enjoy experimenting with them!

< Pesto and Summer Squash Bruschetta

Potstickers

At first glance, potstickers look a little tricky, but don't worry: once you get the knack of pleating, the recipe moves along quickly. If I have extra time, I often make larger batches to freeze and heat as needed. Potstickers make great snacks and appetizers, and I've even been known to eat them for lunch.

As for cooking potstickers, you can choose from a few methods. For an extremely crisp exterior, you can fry the sealed dumplings in oil. If you want to be a bit more health-conscious, baked potstickers will stay crispy, but will be far less oily. My cooking methods for potstickers change, but most of the time I follow the directions as they appear below: essentially, fried in a small amount of oil, then steamed with water.

Vegetable-Loaded Potstickers

YIELD: 18 TO 24 POTSTICKERS

Soy Sauce Mixture
1 tablespoon (15 ml) soy sauce
2 teaspoons honey
1 tablespoon (15 ml) rice wine vinegar

Potstickers
1 cup (70 g) shredded vegetables
2 tablespoons (16 g) sesame seeds
18 to 24 wonton wrappers, square or circle
1 tablespoon (15 ml) sesame or peanut oil
¼ cup (60 ml) water

To make the sauce: In a small bowl, whisk together the soy sauce, honey, and rice wine vinegar.

To make the potstickers: In a separate bowl, combine the shredded vegetables and sesame seeds, then pour the soy sauce mixture over. Toss to combine.

Set up an assembly station with a small bowl of water, the filling, and the wrappers. Working with one wrapper at a time, place about 2 teaspoons of filling in the middle. Dip your finger in the water and run it along the entire edge of the wrapper. Fold both ends up (or corners if using square wrappers) and lightly pinch. Working with one side, pleat and pinch together, making sure that, once pleated, the potsticker is closed. Repeat with the remaining filling and wrappers.

To cook the potstickers, heat the sesame oil over medium-high heat in a large skillet. Place the potstickers in the pan so that no potsticker is touching another. Cook for 1 to 1½ minutes, until the bottom is browned. Pour in the water, place a tight-fitting lid on the pan, and continue to cook for another 2 to 3 minutes, or until the wrappers are tender.

Serve immediately. Cooked potstickers do not store well.

 After the potstickers are assembled, they can easily be frozen. Simply place them on a tray and freeze. Once frozen, transfer to an airtight container. Cook as you would normally, allowing extra time for steaming.

Shredded Bok Choy, Peas, and Ginger Potstickers >

SPRING

Shredded Bok Choy, Peas, and Ginger

YIELD: 18 TO 24 POTSTICKERS

. . . .

1 recipe Vegetable-Loaded Potstickers (page 80)
1 tablespoon (15 ml) olive oil
¾ cup (100 g) green peas
1 teaspoon minced fresh ginger
1½ cups (120 g) finely shredded packed bok choy

Heat a skillet over medium-low heat and add the olive oil. Add the peas and ginger, and cook until the peas are warm, 2 to 3 minutes. Add the bok choy and cook until it starts to wilt, 1 to 2 minutes. Remove the pan from the heat and stir in half the soy sauce mixture from the Vegetable-Loaded Potsticker recipe along with the sesame seeds. Continue with the recipe as directed, using the pea and bok choy mixture as the filling.

 SUMMER

Roasted Zucchini

YIELD: 18 TO 24 POTSTICKERS

. . . .

1 recipe Vegetable-Loaded Potstickers (page 80)
1½ cups (150 g) ¼-inch (6 mm) cubed zucchini
¼ cup (35 g) minced red onion
1 tablespoon (15 ml) olive oil
2 tablespoons (2 g) minced cilantro
½ tablespoon lime juice

Preheat the oven to 400°F (200°C, or gas mark 6). In a roasting pan, toss the zucchini, onion, and olive oil together. Bake until charred, 30 to 35 minutes. Remove from the oven and toss with the cilantro, half the soy sauce mixture (using the lime juice in place of the vinegar), and the sesame seeds from the Vegetable-Loaded Potsticker recipe. Continue with the recipe as directed, using the zucchini mixture as the filling.

FALL

Spicy Acorn Squash

YIELD: 18 TO 24 POTSTICKERS

1 recipe Vegetable-Loaded Potstickers (page 80)
1 acorn squash, sliced in half
1 tablespoon (15 ml) sriracha

Preheat the oven to 425°F (220°C, or gas mark 7). Scoop out the seeds of the acorn squash. Place it cut-side down in a roasting dish and fill the dish with a ¼ inch (6 mm) of water. Bake until the squash is tender, 45 to 50 minutes. Remove from the oven and let cool.

Measure out 1 cup (200 g) of the squash and make the Vegetable-Loaded Potstickers as directed, adding the sriracha to the soy sauce mixture and using the acorn squash as the filling.

 Sweet potato or butternut squash purée also works well in place of the acorn squash.

 WINTER

Brussels Sprouts and Garlic

YIELD: 18 TO 24 POTSTICKERS

1 recipe Vegetable-Loaded Potstickers (page 80)
8 ounces (226 g) Brussels sprouts, ends trimmed
2 cloves garlic, minced
1 tablespoon (15 ml) olive oil

Preheat the oven to 400°F (200°C, or gas mark 6). Bring a pot of water to a boil. Add the trimmed Brussels sprouts and blanch for 4 minutes. Drain, and in a roasting pan, toss the sprouts with the minced garlic and olive oil. Roast for 25 minutes, remove from the oven, and let cool slightly. Pulse the Brussels sprouts in a food processor until broken down. Make the Vegetable-Loaded Potstickers as directed, using the Brussels sprout mixture as the filling.

Hummus

Of all the recipes in this book, this hummus gets the most use. It's my most powerful secret weapon (in the kitchen, at least!), and it's the answer to so many culinary situations. Unexpected house guests arrive hungry? Hummus. Need to add a little bulk to vegetables and rice to make a full meal? Hummus. Want to make that grilled cheese sandwich feel a tad healthier? You guessed it: hummus.

Although hummus appears in the appetizer chapter, I use it more like a condiment: I spread it on my sandwiches, top salads with it, and use it to bind leftover grains and vegetables at lunch or dinner. Sometimes my husband and I make a tapas-style dinner of cheeses, olives, fresh fruit, bread, and a big bowl of hummus. In case you couldn't tell, I absolutely love it.

There are a few techniques for making hummus—especially smooth hummus—such as removing the skin from the beans. I'm a quick-and-dirty kind of cook, so I leave the skins on, but I've found that puréeing all the ingredients before adding the beans helps smooth out the hummus. White beans, such as Great Northern or cannellini beans, also work well in place of the chickpeas.

Traditional Hummus

YIELD: 2 CUPS (480 G)

. . . .

1 clove garlic
¼ cup (56 g) tahini
3 tablespoons (45 ml) lemon juice
3 tablespoons (45 ml) olive oil, plus extra for serving
One 15-ounce (420 g) can chickpeas, drained with juice reserved and rinsed
¼ teaspoon salt
¼ teaspoon pepper, plus extra for serving

In a food processor, pulse the garlic into small pieces. Add the tahini, lemon juice, and olive oil and pulse until well combined. Add the chickpeas, salt, and pepper. Turn on the food processor and let run until smooth, adding the reserved chickpea juice, 1 to 2 tablespoons (15 to 30 ml) at a time, as needed.

Serve with a drizzle of olive oil and a sprinkle of black pepper. Store in an airtight container in the refrigerator for up to a week.

Pumpkin Hummus >

SPRING

Fava Bean

YIELD: 1½ CUPS (360 G)

• •

1 recipe Traditional Hummus (page 84)
1½ cups (270 g) shelled fava beans
2 tablespoons (8 g) chopped flat-leaf parsley

Bring a pot of water to a boil. Add the shelled fava beans and cook for 4 minutes. Drain and remove the outer skins. Make the Traditional Hummus recipe as directed, substituting the fava beans for the chickpeas. Add the parsley with the beans.

 SUMMER

Cilantro Lime

YIELD: 2 CUPS (480 G)

• •

1 recipe Traditional Hummus (page 84)
3 tablespoons (45 ml) lime juice
½ teaspoon lime zest
¼ cup (4 g) packed cilantro
¼ teaspoon smoked paprika

Make the Traditional Hummus as directed, substituting the lime juice for the lemon juice. Once the hummus is smooth, pulse in the lime zest and cilantro until evenly distributed. Serve with the olive oil and a sprinkle of smoked paprika.

 FALL

Pumpkin

YIELD: 2½ CUPS (600 G)

• •

1 recipe Traditional Hummus (page 84)
½ cup (125 g) pumpkin purée
1 chipotle chile in adobo sauce, minced, plus extra for topping
1 tablespoon (15 ml) adobo sauce, plus extra for topping

Make the Traditional Hummus as directed, adding the pumpkin purée, chipotle, and adobo sauce with the tahini, pulsing until smooth. Serve with minced chipotle and a drizzle of the adobo sauce.

 WINTER

Roasted Garlic and Leek

YIELD: 2 CUPS (480 G)

• •

1 recipe Traditional Hummus (page 84)
1 head garlic
2 tablespoons (30 ml) olive oil, divided
1 large leek, white part only

Preheat the oven to 400˚F (200˚C, or gas mark 6). Slice the top off the head of garlic, leaving the cloves slightly exposed. Drizzle 1 tablespoon (15 ml) of the olive oil over the sliced garlic head and wrap in foil. Roast for 35 minutes, until soft. Remove from the oven and let cool. Once cool, squeeze the garlic from the skins. Set aside.

Cut the leek into thin half-moon slices, place in a bowl, and cover with water. Swish the leeks around to remove any dirt, then drain. Heat the remaining 1 tablespoon (15 ml) olive oil in a small skillet over low heat. Add the leeks to the skillet and cook until soft, 5 to 6 minutes.

Make the Traditional Hummus as directed, substituting 7 or 8 cloves roasted garlic and the leeks for the clove of garlic.

Salsa

I won't lie to you: I'm a salsa hoarder. Every summer, I try to can a large batch of salsa to last until the next tomato season, and by the time mid-winter rolls around, I'm usually rationing the precious stuff. Like hummus, I put salsa in the appetizer category here, but it's really more of an all-around condiment. I smother eggs with salsa; use it as a dip for the quesadillas on page 61; and any time I make tacos, I have a batch of salsa close by.

My husband and I take fundamentally different approaches to salsa: he likes it sweet (usually achieved through the addition of pineapple or mango), while I like it savory and spicy. That means I've done a lot of experimenting with salsa varieties. While my favorite is still a simple roasted tomato salsa—a slightly simpler version of the Roasted Tomato and Corn Salsa variation—it's also true that the flavors that come from adding and substituting fruit are really refreshing.

Also, play around with the varieties of tomatoes for the base salsa recipe. I prefer a paste tomato, like the Roma variety, especially when I plan on roasting them first. And as for shelf life, most fresh salsas should keep for up to a week in the refrigerator, so go ahead and make a big batch—especially if you're as much of an addict as I am.

Fresh Tomato Salsa

YIELD: 3 CUPS (780 G)

2 pounds (904 g) Roma tomatoes, diced
½ red onion, diced
1 jalapeño pepper
1 clove garlic, minced
Juice and zest from 1 lime
¼ cup (4 g) minced cilantro
½ teaspoon sea salt

In a bowl, combine the ingredients for the salsa. Toss together and allow the salsa to sit for 1 hour before serving.

SPRING

Radish-Scallion

YIELD: 1½ CUPS (390 G)

. . . .

1 bunch red radishes
4 scallions, minced
1 tablespoon minced jalapeño
2 tablespoons (8 g) minced fresh parsley
1 tablespoon (15 ml) freshly squeezed lemon juice
¼ teaspoon sea salt
⅛ teaspoon black pepper

Cut the radishes into thin slices using a sharp knife or mandoline. Place the ingredients in a bowl and toss until well combined. Allow to sit for 20 minutes before serving.

 SUMMER

Roasted Tomato and Corn

YIELD: 2½ TO 3 CUPS (650 TO 780 G)

. . . .

1 recipe Fresh Tomato Salsa (page 87)
2 ears sweet corn
1 tablespoon (15 ml) olive oil, divided

Preheat the oven to 400°F (200°C, or gas mark 6). Line 2 baking sheets with foil or parchment paper.

Remove the corn from the cob, toss with ½ tablespoon (7.5 ml) of the olive oil, and spread out on a prepared baking sheet. On the other prepared baking sheet, toss together the tomatoes, onion, pepper, and garlic from the original recipe with the remaining ½ tablespoon (7.5 ml) olive oil. Roast the corn for 30 to 35 minutes, until tender, and the tomato mixture for 40 to 50 minutes, until the tomatoes are starting to char. Remove from the oven, and let cool slightly.

Transfer the tomato mixture and the cilantro and lime juice from the original recipe to a food processor and pulse a few times until the tomatoes are broken down. Stir in the roasted corn and serve.

< Cranberry-Lime Salsa

 FALL

Tomatillo

YIELD: 1½ CUPS (390 G)

. . . .

1 pound (452 g) tomatillos
⅓ cup (50 g) diced poblano peppers
½ red onion, diced
1 clove garlic, minced
2 tablespoons (30 ml) lime juice
¼ cup (4 g) cilantro
½ teaspoon salt

Bring a large pot of water to a boil. Add the tomatillos and boil for 2 to 3 minutes. Drain, let cool slightly, and remove the outer skin. Slice the tomatillos into large chunks and place in a food processor along with the remaining ingredients. Process until the salsa is well combined.

 WINTER

Cranberry-Lime

YIELD: 2½ CUPS (650 G)

. . . .

¼ medium red onion
1 jalapeño (14 g), seeded
2 cups (212 g) cranberries
2 mandarin oranges
¼ cup (4 g) chopped cilantro
Juice from 1 lime
¼ teaspoon salt
2 tablespoons (40 g) honey

In a food processor, pulse the onion and jalapeño into small pieces. Add the remaining ingredients, taste, and adjust the flavors as desired.

 Using 1 whole jalapeño results in a pretty spicy salsa. Cut back on the amount if spice isn't your thing.

Crostini

At a party, you'll usually find me hovering around the food. That isn't because I'm super-hungry or antisocial, but because I'm curious: I'm forever looking for inspiration. One thing I notice about party food is, there's nearly always some sort of bread with a topping on offer, and guests go nuts for it. Occasionally it might be bruschetta, like the one on page 100, but other times the toppings are more varied and unique. That's where this crostini comes in. It's a catchall for pretty much anything you can serve on a piece of toasted bread.

The key to this appetizer lies in a good solid base, and in the ratio of the topping to the bread. I prefer a good, whole wheat sourdough baguette, sliced into ¼-inch (6 mm) thick slices. Toppings should be fun and creative, but should be simple enough to whip up relatively quickly.

If I'm looking for a quick, make-ahead appetizer, I usually turn to these crostini. Most of the toppings can be made one or two days ahead, and then assembled closer to serving time. These crostini can also easily be made gluten-free, simply by substituting a good loaf of gluten-free bread. Whichever bread you choose, just be sure to assemble the crostini immediately before serving, otherwise the toast will start to go soft if the topping sits on it for too long.

Easy Crostini

YIELD: 16 TO 20 BREAD SLICES, 4 TO 6 SERVINGS

1 loaf crusty bread or baguette
1 clove garlic, sliced in half
2 tablespoons (30 ml) olive oil

Preheat the broiler. Slice the bread into ¼-inch (6 mm) thick slices. Rub with the sliced end of the garlic and brush with the olive oil. Place under the broiler and toast, 1 to 2 minutes. Remove and top with your favorite ingredients.

SPRING

Cucumber, Mascarpone, and Dill

YIELD: 16 TO 20 BREAD SLICES, 4 TO 6 SERVINGS

. . . .

Cucumbers

1 small cucumber

1 tablespoon (15 ml) olive oil

1 tablespoon (15 ml) lemon juice

1 teaspoon lemon zest

1 clove garlic, minced

Mascarpone Cheese

4 ounces (112 g) mascarpone cheese

2 teaspoons honey

1 tablespoon (2 g) fresh dill, plus extra for topping

⅛ teaspoon sea salt

⅛ teaspoon black pepper

1 recipe Easy Crostini (page 90)

To make the cucumbers: Cut the cucumber into thin slices. Toss with the olive oil, lemon juice, zest, and minced garlic. Cover and let sit for 1 hour.

To make the mascarpone: In a small bowl, combine the cheese, honey, dill, salt, and pepper. Beat with the back of a spoon until smooth and whipped.

Make the Easy Crostini as directed, then spread 1 tablespoon (15 g) of the mascarpone cheese mixture on each slice and top with the marinated cucumbers and a sprinkle of dill.

 SUMMER

Cherry Chutney and Pistachio

YIELD: 16 TO 20 BREAD SLICES, 4 TO 6 SERVINGS

. . . .

1 tablespoon (15 ml) olive oil

¼ cup (35 g) diced red onion

1 teaspoon minced ginger

2 tablespoons (30 ml) apple cider vinegar

1 tablespoon (20 g) molasses

2 cups (310 g) pitted cherries

¼ teaspoon salt

½ teaspoon ground cinnamon

1 teaspoon lemon zest

1 tablespoon (15 ml) freshly squeezed lemon juice

¼ cup (60 ml) water

½ cup (75 g) golden raisins

⅛ teaspoon red pepper flakes (optional)

1 recipe Easy Crostini (page 90)

½ cup (75 g) roasted pistachio pieces

2 ounces (56 g) goat cheese

Heat the oil in a medium saucepan. Add the onion and ginger and cook 3 to 4 minutes. Stir in the vinegar, add the rest of the ingredients through the red pepper flakes (if using), and reduce the heat to medium-low. Let the chutney cook 15 to 20 minutes. Add more water if it's too thick. Remove from the heat and let sit until ready to serve.

Make the Easy Crostini, smear 2 to 3 tablespoons (30 to 45 g) of chutney on each slice, then top with the pistachios and a sprinkle of goat cheese.

FALL

Grape Relish with Honey and Ricotta

YIELD: 16 TO 20 BREAD SLICES, 4 TO 6 SERVINGS

. . . .

1 cup (140 g) green grapes
1 cup (140 g) red grapes
1 tablespoon (20 g) honey
1 teaspoon minced fresh mint
1 tablespoon (15 ml) walnut oil
2 tablespoons (12 g) walnuts
Sea salt
1 cup (240 g) ricotta
1 tablespoon (20 g) honey
1 recipe Easy Crostini (page 90)

Rinse the grapes, slice in half, and add to a bowl. Add the honey, mint, walnut oil, walnuts, and sea salt and toss to combine.

In a separate bowl, stir together the ricotta and honey.

Make the Easy Crostini as directed, then spread 1 to 2 table-spoons (15 to 30 g) of ricotta on each slice and top with the grape mixture.

 The grape mixture can be made up to a day in advance and refrigerated until ready to use.

 WINTER

Roasted Garlic and Goat Cheese with Parsley Pesto

YIELD: 16 TO 20 BREAD SLICES, 4 TO 6 SERVINGS

. . . .

Topping
1 ounce (28 g) cream cheese, at room temperature
4 ounces (112 g) goat cheese, at room temperature
6 cloves roasted garlic (page 86)
¼ cup (60 ml) heavy cream
¼ teaspoon sea salt
¼ teaspoon black pepper
Drizzle of honey

Parsley Pesto
1 cup (60) parsley
2 tablespoons (30 ml) olive oil
2 tablespoons (30 ml) lemon juice
1 tablespoon (9 g) toasted pine nuts, plus more for garnish

1 recipe Easy Crostini (page 90)

To make the topping: In a bowl, beat together the ingredients for the topping until well combined and fluffy.

To make the pesto: In a small food processor, place the ingredients for the parsley pesto and process until well combined.

Make the Easy Crostini as directed, then smear 2 to 3 table-spoons (30 to 45 g) of the cream cheese mixture on each slice and top with a drizzle of parsley pesto and a sprinkle of chopped pine nuts.

Spring Rolls

Like potstickers, spring rolls aren't terribly hard to make once you master your wrapping technique and learn how to work with the wet rice paper. It might take a little trial and error, but I've found that leaving the wrapper in the water just until it starts to get soft and then placing it on the cutting board works best. The softer the rice paper, the harder it is to transfer. The rice paper will continue to soften as you layer on your filling.

The only downside to spring rolls is that they're not the best make-ahead appetizers. The wrappers will begin to lose moisture and dry out, toughening up their exteriors: this can be (partially) avoided by wrapping any extra spring rolls in a damp paper towel and storing them in an airtight container in the refrigerator. Keeping the rice paper moist is the key to storing them so they'll remain pliable. Most health food stores and Asian markets sell the rice papers. Occasionally, I find brown rice papers, which I prefer over their white counterparts.

Fresh Spring Rolls

YIELD: 8 TO 10 SPRING ROLLS

. . . .

6 ounces (168 g) brown rice noodles
8 to 10 rice papers
3 to 4 cups (300 to 400 g) shredded or
   matchstick vegetables

Soy-Ginger Dipping Sauce
3 tablespoons (45 ml) soy sauce
2 tablespoons (30 ml) rice wine vinegar
2 teaspoons hoisin sauce
1 teaspoon minced fresh ginger
1 teaspoon sriracha

Cook the noodles according to the package directions. Drain and rinse under cool water.

Set up an assembly station with the cooked noodles, rice papers, vegetables, a dish of hot water large enough to hold the spring roll wrappers, and a cutting board.

Soak the rice paper for 10 to 15 seconds, until pliable but not extremely soft. (Soaking time may be longer or shorter depending on water temperature.) Place the wrapper on the cutting board and add ⅓ cup (45 g) cooked noodles and roughly ½ cup (50 g) vegetables, laying them slightly off-center, toward you. Fold the wrapper edge closest to you over the filling, tucking the edge under the filling. Fold the sides over and continue to roll away from you. Repeat with the remaining ingredients.

To make the sauce: Place all the ingredients in a small bowl and whisk to combine. Serve with the spring rolls.

 Spring roll wrappers come in different shapes, such as circular and square, as well as white and brown rice papers. I usually use brown rice wrappers in whichever shape I can get at the time. Try a couple of different varieties, and decide on your favorites!

SPRING

Roasted Sesame Scallion

YIELD: 8 TO 10 SPRING ROLLS

. . . .

1 recipe Fresh Spring Rolls (page 93)
1 bunch scallions
1 tablespoon (15 ml) olive oil
1 teaspoon honey
1 tablespoon (8 g) sesame seeds
2 cups (80 g) micro greens

Preheat the oven to 375°F (190°C, or gas mark 5). Wash the scallions and trim off the bottom and part of the green tops, leaving the white and 3 to 4 inches (7.5 to 10 cm) of the greens. Slice each scallion in half horizontally and each half into 2 or 3 lengthwise strips. Place in a roasting pan and toss with the olive oil, honey, and sesame seeds. Roast until tender and lightly browned, 15 to 20 minutes.

Make the Fresh Spring Rolls as directed, adding the roasted scallions and micro greens to the filling; serve with the Soy-Ginger Dipping Sauce.

 SUMMER

Marinated Cucumber Noodles

YIELD: 8 TO 10 SPRING ROLLS

. . . .

1 recipe Fresh Spring Rolls (page 93)
1 large cucumber
½ red onion, thinly sliced
1 teaspoon black pepper
½ teaspoon mustard powder
⅛ teaspoon fennel powder
⅛ teaspoon ground cloves
¼ to ½ teaspoon red pepper flakes
½ cup (120 ml) water
3 tablespoons (45 ml) white vinegar
1 teaspoon sea salt

Using a spiralizer or julienne peeler, cut the cucumber into noodles. Combine the cucumber noodles, onion slices, and spices in an airtight container.

In a small saucepan, bring the water, vinegar, and salt to a boil. Remove from the heat and pour over the cucumber noodles. Let cool, reseal the container, and refrigerate overnight.

Make the Fresh Spring Rolls as directed, adding the cucumber noodles to the filling; serve with the Soy-Ginger Dipping Sauce.

 If you don't own a spiralizer or julienne peeler, use a vegetable peeler on the cucumbers, then cut the strips into thin noodles.

Grilled Sweet Potato with Cilantro Sauce

YIELD: 8 TO 10 SPRING ROLLS

Sweet Potato
1 large sweet potato
1 tablespoon (14 g) coconut oil, melted
¼ teaspoon sea salt
½ teaspoon ground cumin

Cilantro Sauce
2 tablespoons (30 ml) coconut milk
¼ cup (4 g) cilantro
½ teaspoon minced fresh ginger
½ teaspoon minced garlic
2 tablespoons (30 ml) freshly squeezed lime juice

1 recipe Fresh Spring Rolls (page 93)

To make the sweet potato: Light the grill. Peel the sweet potato and cut lengthwise into ¼-inch (6 mm) thick slices. Bring a pot of water to a boil and add the sweet potato slices. Cook for 4 minutes, drain, and toss with the coconut oil, salt, and cumin. Grill for 5 to 6 minutes on each side. Remove from the heat and let cool slightly. Cut into matchsticks.

To make the sauce: In a small bowl, combine the ingredients for the cilantro sauce and whisk until blended.

Make the Fresh Spring Rolls as directed, adding the sweet potato to the filling and combining the cilantro sauce with the noodles before assembling. Serve with or without the dipping sauce.

Celery Root and Kale with Peanut Sauce

YIELD: 8 TO 10 SPRING ROLLS

1 recipe Fresh Spring Rolls (page 93)
1 large celery root, peeled and cut into matchsticks
1 tablespoon (15 ml) olive oil
2 cups (80 g) shredded kale
1 recipe Peanut Sauce (page 48)

Preheat oven to 400°F (200°C, or gas mark 6). Toss the celery root with the olive oil and spread in a single layer on a baking sheet. Roast until tender, 25 to 30 minutes.

Drain the noodles from the Fresh Spring Rolls recipe and, instead of rinsing, toss with the kale and let sit until the kale is slightly wilted. Make the Spring Rolls as directed, using the celery root and noodle-kale mixture as the filling; serve with the peanut sauce.

Savory Turnovers

If you'd told me as a child that turnovers could have savory fillings, I'd have laughed at you and gone right on munching my sweet cherry or apple pastry. The local bakery sold perfectly flaky turnovers that were always decked out with an extra-special touch of icing drizzle. Then, when I worked at the bakery, making turnovers became my job, and that was when I was first introduced to the idea of a savory pastry in the form of spinach and cheese. That combination completely changed my perspective on baked goods.

These turnovers use a base similar to my favorite pie crust, and the whole wheat pastry flour is crucial for keeping the dough light. However, if you can't find whole wheat pastry flour, unbleached all-purpose flour will work as well. For an extra-special treat, smear a bit of cream cheese in the center of each turnover before adding the filling.

To make these turnovers ahead of time, prepare them all the way through, just until they're ready to bake, then refrigerate them until you're ready to use them, or freeze them for extended storage (making sure, in both instances, that the filling is cooled before assembling). I make the larger versions if I'm looking for a decent-size snack, and the smaller turnovers if I'm in need of a good party appetizer.

Whole Wheat Turnovers

YIELD: 8 LARGE OR 12 SMALL TURNOVERS

1½ cups (180 g) whole wheat pastry flour
½ teaspoon sea salt
½ cup (112 g) cold unsalted butter
2 tablespoons (30 ml) maple syrup
2 to 3 tablespoons (30 to 45 ml) cold water
1 cup (250 g) filling of choice

Egg Wash
1 large egg
1 tablespoon (15 ml) heavy cream

Combine the flour and salt in a bowl. Using your hands or a pastry blender, cut the cold butter into the flour mixture until the mixture resembles coarse meal. Add the maple syrup and 2 tablespoons (30 ml) of the water, stirring until a soft ball forms, adding the remaining 1 tablespoon (15 ml) water as needed. Wrap and place in the refrigerator for 15 minutes.

Preheat the oven to 375°F (190°C, or gas mark 5). Line a baking sheet with parchment paper.

Remove the dough from the refrigerator and divide in half. Turn out onto a floured surface and roll into a 12 by 16-inch (30 by 40 cm) rectangle, and then cut into 8 large (4 by 6-inch, or 10 by 15 cm) or 12 small (3 by 4-inch, or 7.5 by 10 cm) rectangles. Divide the filling among the rectangles, placing it in the middle. Take one corner and fold it over the filling, then seal the edges with a fork. Repeat with the remaining dough and filling. Place on the prepared baking sheet.

To make the egg wash: Beat together the egg and heavy cream and brush the top of each turnover with the egg wash. Bake for 26 to 30 minutes, until golden. Let cool before serving. Store extra turnovers in an airtight container at room temperature, or freeze for extended storage.

Spiced Chickpea and Root Vegetable Turnovers >

SPRING

Spicy Rhubarb Lentil

YIELD: 8 LARGE OR 12 SMALL TURNOVERS

. . . .

Filling

1 cup (110 g) diced rhubarb
¾ cup (134 g) dried green lentils
1½ cups (360 ml) vegetable broth
1 teaspoon minced ginger
⅛ teaspoon red pepper flakes
4 Medjool dates, pitted
1 clove garlic, minced

1 recipe Whole Wheat Turnovers (page 96)

To make the filling: Combine all the filling ingredients in a pot. Bring to a boil, reduce to a simmer, and cook until the lentils are tender and the vegetable broth has been absorbed, 22 to 25 minutes. Remove from the heat and lightly mash.

Make the Whole Wheat Turnovers as directed, using the mashed lentils as the filling.

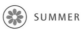 SUMMER

Sweet Corn and Cream Cheese

YIELD: 8 LARGE OR 12 SMALL TURNOVERS

. . . .

Filling

½ tablespoon olive oil
2 ears sweet corn, kernels removed
1 clove garlic, minced
1 tablespoon (1.7 g) minced fresh rosemary
¼ teaspoon sea salt
¼ teaspoon black pepper
1 tablespoon (15 ml) heavy cream
3 ounces (84 g) cream cheese, at room temperature

1 recipe Whole Wheat Turnovers (page 96)

To make the filling: Heat the olive oil in a skillet and add the corn kernels. Cook until tender, 4 to 5 minutes. Stir in the garlic, rosemary, sea salt, and black pepper, and cook 1 minute more. Remove from the heat and let cool.

In a food processor, combine the heavy cream and cream cheese, pulsing until the cream cheese is fluffy. Add the roasted corn mixture, pulsing until just combined. Make the Whole Wheat Turnovers as directed using the corn filling.

FALL

Curried Potato and Roasted Garlic

YIELD: 8 LARGE OR 12 SMALL TURNOVERS

• •

Filling

8 ounces (226 g) red potatoes, quartered

4 or 5 cloves garlic, roasted (page 86)

2 tablespoons (30 ml) coconut milk

1 tablespoon (6 g) curry powder

1 recipe Whole Wheat Turnovers (page 96)

To make the filling: Bring a pot of water to a boil and add the potatoes. Cook until tender but not falling apart, 5 to 6 minutes. Drain and place in a bowl. Add the roasted garlic cloves, and stir to combine. In a small bowl, mix together the coconut milk and curry powder. Add to the potatoes and roasted garlic, tossing and mashing slightly.

Make the Whole Wheat Turnovers as directed, using the potato filling.

 WINTER

Spiced Chickpea and Root Vegetable

YIELD: 8 LARGE OR 12 SMALL TURNOVERS

• •

Filling

½ cup (60 g) peeled, cubed rutabaga

½ cup (60 g) peeled, cubed parsnips

½ cup (60 g) peeled, cubed turnips

½ cup (65 g) chickpeas

1 tablespoon (15 ml) freshly squeezed lime juice

½ teaspoon ground cumin

½ teaspoon ground coriander

¼ teaspoon salt

¼ teaspoon pepper

1 recipe Whole Wheat Turnovers (page 96)

To make the filling: Bring a pot of water to a boil and add the cubed root vegetables. Cook until tender, 12 to 15 minutes. Drain and transfer to a bowl. Stir in the chickpeas, lime juice, cumin, coriander, salt, and pepper. Using a fork or potato masher, mash the mixture until well combined.

Make the Whole Wheat Turnovers as directed, using the root vegetable filling.

Bruschetta

If you were to cook with me in my kitchen, there are a few things you'd notice right away. For starters, I'm extremely messy, even after years of teaching myself to clean as I go. I'm also usually disorganized, which means I end up doing laps around the kitchen. And—unless I'm working—"recipe" is a word I seldom use. Instead, I much prefer to wing it, tasting and adjusting as I go. It's more fun, and besides, some things just don't require recipes.

Bruschetta is one of those things. During the summer, with its abundance of tomatoes, I'll often throw together a batch without measuring the tomatoes, guessing on the quantities of basil and olive oil, and relying on taste to get the seasonings just right. It's low-fuss cooking at its best: fresh produce and vibrant, minimalist flavors.

You've probably had your fair share of bruschetta, as it seems to be a popular menu item at restaurants. But it's easy to make at home, and it comes together very quickly. The variations here diverge from the original recipe, but the fresh-produce-minimalist-flavor concept is still very much there in each of them. As always, experiment with the flavors, and if you have any leftover bruschetta topping, use it up in an omelet (page 30) or slathered onto a grilled cheese sandwich (page 51).

Basic Bruschetta

YIELD: 4 TO 6 SERVINGS

. . . .

Topping
1 pound (454 g) Roma tomatoes, chopped
3 tablespoons (7.5 g) fresh basil, julienned
1 clove garlic, minced
1 tablespoon (15 ml) olive oil
2 teaspoons balsamic vinegar
¼ teaspoon black pepper
¼ teaspoon sea salt

Bread
1 small baguette
2 tablespoons (15 ml) olive oil
¼ teaspoon black pepper

To make the topping: In a bowl, combine the chopped tomatoes, basil, garlic, olive oil, balsamic vinegar, pepper, and sea salt. Cover and let sit for 30 minutes.

To make the bread: Preheat the broiler. Cut the bread on the diagonal into ½-inch (1.3 cm) thick slices. Place on a baking sheet, brush each slice with olive oil, and add a sprinkle of black pepper. Place the tray under the broiler and lightly toast, 30 to 60 seconds.

Remove the bread slices, top each with a hefty spoonful of the tomato mixture, and serve. The tomato mixture can be made the day before and stored in the refrigerator until ready to use.

SPRING

Roasted Radish and Herb

YIELD: 2 TO 3 SERVINGS

. . . .

Topping

8 ounces (226 g) French breakfast radishes

2 shallots, thinly sliced

1 tablespoon (15 ml) olive oil, divided

¼ teaspoon salt

¼ teaspoon pepper

1 teaspoon minced fresh parsley

1 teaspoon minced fresh thyme

1 teaspoon chopped fresh chives

1 teaspoon freshly squeezed lemon juice

½ recipe Basic Bruschetta Bread (page 100)

To make the topping: Preheat the oven to 375°F (190°C, or gas mark 5) Slice the radishes in half lengthwise, then cut each half into ¼-inch (6 mm) thick half-moons. Toss with the sliced shallots, ½ tablespoon (7.5 ml) of the olive oil, salt, and pepper. Spread in a roasting pan and bake until tender, 20 to 25 minutes. Remove from the oven and toss with the remaining ½ tablespoon (7.5 ml) olive oil, minced herbs, and lemon juice.

Make the Basic Bruschetta Bread as directed, and serve topped with the warm radish mixture.

 SUMMER

Pesto and Summer Squash

YIELD: 4 TO 6 SERVINGS

. . . .

Squash

1 medium yellow summer squash, ends cut

¼ red onion, sliced

½ tablespoon olive oil

¼ teaspoon black pepper

Pesto

2 cloves garlic

1½ cups (60 g) packed basil leaves

⅓ cup (33 g) Parmesan cheese

2 tablespoons (18 g) toasted pine nuts

¼ cup (60 ml) olive oil

3 tablespoons (45 ml) freshly squeezed lemon juice

1 recipe Basic Bruschetta Bread (page 100)

1 to 2 ounces (28 to 56 g) feta cheese, for serving

To make the squash: Light the grill to medium-high heat. Slice the squash into ½-inch (1.3 cm) slices. Brush the squash and onion with the olive oil and sprinkle with the pepper. Grill 2 to 3 minutes per side. Remove from the grill, let cool slightly, cut the squash into cubes, and dice the onion.

To make the pesto: In a food processor, pulse the garlic. Add the basil, Parmesan, pine nuts, olive oil, and lemon juice. Pulse until well combined, adding more liquid as needed to thin the consistency. Toss the squash mixture with ¼ cup (60 g) of the pesto.

Make the Basic Bruschetta Bread as directed and top with the warm pesto squash and a sprinkling of feta cheese.

FALL

Pumpkin, Pistachio, and Crispy Sage

YIELD: 4 TO 6 SERVINGS

Pumpkin

3 cups (360 g) cubed pumpkin
½ cup (60 g) diced red onion
1 tablespoon (15 ml) olive oil
1 tablespoon (20 g) honey
¼ teaspoon sea salt
¼ teaspoon black pepper

Pistachios

½ tablespoon olive oil
3 or 4 fresh sage leaves
¼ cup (30 g) roasted, unsalted pistachios

1 recipe Basic Bruschetta Bread (page 100)

To make the pumpkin: Preheat the oven to 400°F (200°C, or gas mark 6). In a roasting pan, toss the pumpkin with the red onion, olive oil, honey, sea salt, and black pepper. Roast until tender, 25 to 30 minutes.

To make the pistachios: In a small skillet, heat the olive oil over medium-low heat and add the sage leaves. Fry until crisp, 1 to 2 minutes. Remove the sage from the pan and place in a food processor with the pistachios. Pulse until the pistachios are in small, meal-like pieces. Toss the roasted pumpkin mixture with the pistachio mixture until well combined.

Make the Basic Bruschetta Bread as directed and top with the roasted pumpkin-pistachio mixture.

 WINTER

Parsnip and Rutabaga

YIELD: 4 TO 6 SERVINGS

Topping

1 parsnip
1 rutabaga
1 tablespoon (15 ml) olive oil
1 clove garlic, minced
2 tablespoons (18 g) finely chopped walnuts
2 teaspoons balsamic vinegar
2 teaspoons maple syrup

1 recipe Basic Bruschetta Bread (page 100)

To make the topping: Preheat the oven to 400°F (200°C, or gas mark 6). Peel the parsnip and rutabaga, then cut into ¼-inch (6 mm) cubes. Toss with the olive oil and minced garlic, then place in a roasting pan. Roast for 35 to 40 minutes, until tender. Remove from the oven and toss with the walnuts, balsamic vinegar, and maple syrup.

Make the Basic Bruschetta Bread as directed and top with the root vegetable mixture.

Vegetable Skewers

Not long ago, my husband and I spent the evening walking around an amusement park. We were starving, and the only food that sounded halfway decent came in the form of a skewer. I ordered a vegetarian skewer, and was presented with nothing more than barely cooked vegetables with a wedge of lime, salt, and pepper. I was disappointed, to say the least.

But that evening had a silver lining: after that, I started experimenting with different versions of grilled vegetable skewers at home. After all, why suffer through bland vegetables when even simple additions such as olive oil, garlic, salt, and pepper can really dress up their flavors? Done well, vegetable skewers make for a great, light appetizer, or they can be used as a base for a meal by adding protein, such as tofu, or by serving them over a bed of grains.

Since we grill quite a bit, I invested in a set of nice metal skewers, but you can, of course, also use wood skewers. To use wood skewers, soak them in water for at least an hour before using: this will keep them from catching fire on the grill. Also, if you're worried that the skewers might stick, using a grill plate is a simple solution.

Versatile Vegetable Skewers

YIELD: 2 TO 3 SERVINGS

3 cups (480 g) 1-inch (2.5 cm) assorted cubed
   vegetables
2 tablespoons (30 ml) olive oil
2 cloves garlic, minced
1 tablespoon (15 ml) freshly squeezed lemon juice
½ teaspoon sea salt
¼ teaspoon black pepper

If using wood skewers, soak in water for at least an hour before using.

In a bowl, toss together the cubed vegetables, olive oil, garlic, lemon juice, salt, and pepper. Cover and let sit while the grill preheats.

Preheat the grill to medium-low. Thread the cubed vegetables onto the skewers, alternating vegetables until the skewer is three-fourths full. Place on the grill and cook until the vegetables are starting to char, rotating every 3 to 4 minutes. Remove from the grill and serve.

SPRING

Mustard-Grilled Beets

YIELD: 2 TO 3 SERVINGS

. . . .

1 pound (454 g) beets (red, yellow, or Chioggia)
2 tablespoons (30 ml) olive oil, divided
¼ teaspoon salt
¼ teaspoon pepper
1 tablespoon (11 g) stone-ground brown mustard
1 tablespoon (20 g) honey
1 tablespoon (15 ml) apple cider vinegar

Preheat the oven to 375˚F (190˚C, or gas mark 5). Scrub the beets, then toss them with 1 tablespoon (15 ml) of the olive oil and place in a roasting pan. Cover with foil and bake until tender, 45 to 50 minutes. Remove from the oven and let cool slightly. Once ready to handle, peel the beets and cut into ½-inch (1.3 cm) cubes.

Whisk together the remaining 1 tablespoon (15 ml) oil, salt, pepper, mustard, honey, and vinegar. Thread the beets onto skewers and lay the skewers in a baking dish. Brush with the marinade, cover, and let sit for 2 to 3 hours.

If using wood skewers, soak in water for at least an hour before using.

Preheat the grill to medium-low. Brush the beets again with the marinade, and place on the grill. Grill, rotating and brushing with the marinade, until lightly browned, 3 to 4 minutes on each side. Remove from the grill and brush once more with the marinade. Serve hot.

 SUMMER

Jerk Zucchini

YIELD: 2 TO 3 SERVINGS

. . . .

1 recipe Versatile Vegetable Skewers (page 103)
1 medium zucchini
1 small red onion
2 teaspoons jerk seasoning

If using wood skewers, soak in water for at least an hour before using.

Preheat the grill to medium-low. Trim the ends off the zucchini and cut in half lengthwise. Slice each half into ½-inch (1.3 cm) half-moon slices. Make the Versatile Vegetable Skewers as directed, adding the jerk seasoning in with the other ingredients and reducing the olive oil to 1 tablespoon (15 ml).

FALL

Mushroom and Onion

YIELD: 3 SERVINGS

. . . .

9 white button mushrooms (roughly ½ pound [224 g])
1 small red onion, cut into mushroom size chunks
¼ cup (60 ml) olive oil, divided
¼ teaspoon sea salt
¼ teaspoon black pepper
1 teaspoon minced fresh parsley, plus extra for serving
1 teaspoon minced fresh oregano
1 teaspoon minced fresh thyme

If using wood skewers, soak in water for at least an hour before using.

Preheat the grill to medium-low. Thread 3 mushrooms and onion chunks, alternating vegetables, onto each of 3 skewers. Brush with 2 tablespoons (30 ml) of the olive oil, sprinkle with salt and pepper, and grill until lightly charred, 3 to 4 minutes per side. Mix together the remaining 2 tablespoons (30 ml) olive oil and the herbs. Remove the skewers from the grill and brush with the herb mixture. Serve.

 WINTER

Turnips with Dill Olive Oil

YIELD: 2 TO 3 SERVINGS

. . . .

Turnips
1 large turnip, cubed
1 tablespoon (15 ml) olive oil
½ teaspoon sea salt
¼ teaspoon black pepper

Dill Oil
2 teaspoons minced fresh dill
1 tablespoon (15 ml) olive oil
1 tablespoon (15 ml) lemon juice
¼ teaspoon salt

If using wood skewers, soak in water for at least an hour before using.

To make the turnips: Bring a pot of water to a boil over high heat, add the turnips, and cook for 2 minutes. Drain, add to a bowl, and toss with the olive oil, salt, and pepper.

Preheat the grill to medium-low. Thread the turnips onto skewers and grill until lightly charred, 2 to 3 minutes on each side.

To make the dill oil: Combine all the ingredients in a bowl and whisk together. Drizzle the dill oil over the grilled turnips and serve while still hot.

Baked Cheese and Chutney

Both my husband and I love cheese—probably a little too much. Some weekends, we like to make a special trip to the store to grab an assortment of cheeses, olives, crackers, and fruit. Then we head home to make our own little cheese platter for dinner. For movie nights, I'm likely to whip up some kind of cheese-related treat, whether it's a spinach-and-artichoke dip or one of the baked cheese variations listed here.

The idea for the cheese and chutney combination actually comes from a relatively easy version of cheese and salsa that my husband's mother used to serve us when we stopped by. I loved the way the salsa's spicy flavor contrasted with the cheese (which, in this case, was cream cheese). I transferred this idea to chutney, one of my favorite condiments. Then I decided that applying it to all kinds of cheese would be a great idea, because really, why stop at just one?

I've tucked chutney into this chapter, but it deserves to be used in many more ways, like with the grilled polenta on page 58 or the crostini with cherry chutney on page 91. It's an easy condiment to throw together, and it'll keep in the refrigerator for up to a week. Be sure to use fresh ginger and good lemon zest. Both flavors, even though they're only used in small amounts, really make the chutney.

Cheese and Ginger Chutney

YIELD: 4 TO 6 SERVINGS

Chutney
1 tablespoon (15 ml) olive oil
¼ cup (35 g) diced red onion
1 teaspoon minced fresh ginger
2 tablespoons (30 ml) apple cider vinegar
2 cups (360 g) diced tomatoes (or fruit)
¼ cup (48 g) pitted and chopped Medjool dates
⅓ cup (50 g) golden raisins
1 tablespoon (15 ml) lemon juice
1 teaspoon lemon zest
½ teaspoon ground cinnamon
¼ teaspoon salt
¼ cup (60 ml) water, or more as needed
¼ teaspoon red pepper flakes (optional)

4 to 6 ounces (112 to 168 g) cheese,
   such as goat or Brie
Sliced bread, pita, or crackers, for serving

To make the chutney: In a medium saucepan, heat the olive oil. Add the onion and ginger and cook until fragrant, 3 to 4 minutes. Stir in the vinegar, then add the remaining ingredients and reduce the heat to medium-low. Cook until the tomatoes and dates have broken down into a chunky sauce, 15 to 20 minutes. Add more water if the chutney is too thick. Remove from the heat and let sit until ready to serve.

Preheat the oven as directed in the seasonal variations that follow. Place the cheese in an ovenproof dish and bake until warm and soft. Cover the warm cheese with the chutney and serve with sliced bread, pita, or crackers.

SPRING

Rhubarb Chutney with Baked Ricotta

YIELD: 4 TO 6 SERVINGS

· ·

1 recipe Cheese and Ginger Chutney (page 106)
2 cups (220 g) diced rhubarb
¼ cup (24 g) minced scallion
1 cup (240 g) whole-milk ricotta
2 ounces (56 g) fontina cheese, shredded
1 large egg white
2 tablespoons (20 g) minced garlic scapes
¼ teaspoon salt
¼ teaspoon black pepper
Sliced almonds, for topping

Prepare the chutney as directed, using the rhubarb as the fruit and the scallions in place of the red onion.

Preheat the oven to 375°F (190°C, or gas mark 5). In a food processor, combine the ricotta, fontina cheese, egg white, garlic scapes, salt, and pepper. Purée until well combined. Scoop the ricotta into a small baking dish and smooth the top with the back of a spoon. Bake until the ricotta has puffed up and is lightly brown, 25 to 28 minutes.

Remove the ricotta from the oven and cover with the chutney. Top with the sliced almonds. Serve immediately.

 SUMMER

Blackberry Chutney with Cream Cheese

YIELD: 4 TO 6 SERVINGS

· ·

1 recipe Cheese and Ginger Chutney (page 106)
2 cups (280 g) blackberries
1 tablespoon (6 g) minced fresh ginger
One 8-ounce (226 g) package cream cheese, softened
2 ounces (56 g) shredded fontina or Havarti cheese
2 tablespoons (30 ml) milk
¼ teaspoon salt
¼ teaspoon pepper
1 tablespoon (20 g) honey

Prepare the chutney recipe as directed, using the blackberries as the fruit and increasing the amount of ginger to 1 table-spoon (6 g).

Preheat the oven to 375°F (190°C, or gas mark 5). In a food processor, combine the cream cheese, shredded cheese, milk, salt, pepper, and honey. Pulse until smooth. Scoop into a small baking dish and smooth the top with the back of a spoon. Bake for 15 to 20 minutes, until the cheese is soft and lightly browning. Remove from the oven, cover with the blackberry chutney, and serve.

FALL

Baked Goat Cheese with Apple Chutney

YIELD: 4 TO 6 SERVINGS

. . . .

1 recipe Cheese and Ginger Chutney (page 106)
2 cups (220 g) peeled and diced apples
2 tablespoons (30 ml) maple syrup
4 ounces (112 g) goat cheese

Prepare the chutney as directed, using the apples as the fruit and replacing the dates with the maple syrup.

Preheat the oven to 350°F (180°C, or gas mark 4). Divide the goat cheese into four 1-ounce (28 g) pieces. Place in a baking dish and cover with the chutney. Bake until the goat cheese is soft, 20 to 25 minutes.

 WINTER

Baked Brie with Meyer Lemon Vinaigrette

YIELD: 4 TO 6 SERVINGS

. . . .

One 8-ounce (226 g) wheel Brie

Vinaigrette
1 Meyer lemon
2 tablespoons (30 ml) olive oil
1 tablespoon (15 ml) champagne vinegar
1 tablespoon (20 g) honey
¼ teaspoon sea salt
¼ teaspoon black pepper

Preheat the oven to 375°F (190°C, or gas mark 5). Line a small, circular baking pan with parchment paper. Place the wheel of Brie in the baking dish and cook until the cheese has melted, 8 to 10 minutes.

To make the vinaigrette: Zest the Meyer lemon into a bowl, then peel. Remove the pith and seeds from the lemon slices. Roughly chop the lemon and add to the bowl, lightly squeezing out some of the juice as well. Whisk in the remaining ingredients. Pour the lemon vinaigrette over the baked Brie and serve.

Flatbread

When I began to move away from using strict recipes, it was more out of necessity than anything else. Living in a small, rural town had its advantages, but a large selection of whole foods wasn't one of them. Eventually, I learned to make recipes work according to what I had on hand at the time. For instance, once I was about to cook for a party, and I'd planned to make a version of the crostini on page 90. I reached for the baguette I had purchased—only to find it hard as a rock. A quick run to the two grocery stores in town ensued, but neither of them had any more baguettes. So instead of changing my plans altogether, I whipped up an early version of this flatbread.

Over the years, what started out as a crisp, cracker-like crust morphed into a pliable, soft flatbread that's perfect for piling on the ingredients. I prefer using 100 percent white whole wheat flour, but the resulting dough isn't always the easiest to work with when it comes to rolling it out, so a mixture of the wheat flour and unbleached all-purpose flour works best.

As for toppings, go crazy! Many of the toppings in the crostini (page 90) and bruschetta (page 100) sections would work well with this flatbread, or you could even serve the hummus (page 84) with grilled chunks of the bread. The dough freezes well, too, and I usually end up freezing half the dough and thawing it later as part of a quick meal.

Quick Flatbread

YIELD. 4 TO 6 SERVINGS

. . . .

1½ cups (180 g) white wheat or unbleached
    all-purpose flour
½ teaspoon sea salt
2 teaspoons baking powder
3 tablespoons (45 ml) olive oil
1 tablespoon (20 g) honey
6 tablespoons (90 ml) warm water

In a large bowl, whisk together the flour, sea salt, and baking powder. Using your fingers or a fork, blend the olive oil into the flour until the flour mixture looks shaggy. In a separate bowl, whisk together the honey and warm water. Pour the wet ingredients into the flour mixture, and stir until a dough forms. Cover and let rest for 30 minutes.

Heat a griddle over medium-low heat. Divide the dough into 2 pieces (rough 150 g each) and roll each into a 6 by 8 inch (15 by 20 cm) rectangle. Cook for 3 minutes, flip, then cook for another 2 to 3 minutes, until lightly brown.

Top with vegetables, olive oil, herbs, and/or cheese (see variations that follow), and serve. Store leftovers in an airtight container in the refrigerator for up to 2 days.

 Flatbread dough can be frozen and thawed when ready to use.

SPRING

Shaved Asparagus

YIELD: 4 TO 6 SERVINGS

1 recipe Quick Flatbread (page 109)
2 tablespoons (30 ml) olive oil
Zest from 1 lemon
1 clove garlic, minced
8 ounces (226 g) asparagus
4 ounces (112 g) mozzarella cheese

Make the Quick Flatbread as directed. Preheat the broiler.

In a small bowl, whisk together the olive oil, lemon zest, and garlic. Place the finished flatbreads on a baking tray and brush each with the olive oil mixture.

Using a vegetable peeler, shave the asparagus into thin ribbons. Spread on the flatbread and finish with 2 ounces (56 g) shredded mozzarella cheese per flatbread. Place the flatbread under the broiler until the cheese has melted, 60 to 90 seconds.

 SUMMER

Herbed Grilled Zucchini

YIELD: 4 TO 6 SERVINGS

1 recipe Quick Flatbread (page 109)
2 medium-size zucchini, cut into ¼-inch (6 mm) strips
¼ cup (56 g) plain Greek yogurt
2 tablespoons (12 g) herbes de Provence
3 ounces (84 g) crumbled feta

Prepare the Quick Flatbread as directed. Preheat the grill.

In a bowl, toss together the zucchini, yogurt, and herbes de Provence. Place the zucchini strips on the grill and cook until starting to brown, 2 to 3 minutes per side. Remove from the grill and let cool slightly. Cut the strips into cubes and toss with the crumbled feta. Top the flatbread with the zucchini and feta mixture and serve.

FALL

Hazelnut, Apple, and Manchego Cheese

YIELD: 4 TO 6 SERVINGS

. . . .

1 recipe Quick Flatbread (page 109)
2 tablespoons (30 ml) olive oil
4 teaspoons fresh thyme
1 apple, cut into ¼ inch (6 mm) slices
2 ounces (56 g) toasted hazelnuts
4 ounces (112 g) shredded Manchego cheese

Prepare the Quick Flatbread as directed. Preheat the broiler.

In a small saucepan, heat the olive oil and thyme over low heat just until the oil is warm. Remove from the heat and let cool.

Place the flatbreads on a baking tray and spread the apple slices on top. Sprinkle on the toasted hazelnuts and Manchego cheese. Broil for 2 to 3 minutes, watching carefully, until the cheese has melted and is starting to bubble and brown. Remove from the oven, let cool for 1 minute, and finish with a drizzle of thyme oil.

 WINTER

Roasted Garlic, Rosemary, and Goat Cheese

YIELD: 4 TO 6 SERVINGS

. . . .

1 recipe Quick Flatbread (page 109)
2 tablespoons (30 ml) olive oil, plus more for serving
6 to 8 cloves roasted garlic (page 86)
2 teaspoons minced fresh rosemary
4 ounces (112 g) crumbled goat cheese

Prepare the Quick Flatbread as directed. Preheat the broiler.

Place the finished flatbreads on a baking sheet and brush with the olive oil, then, with a knife, smear the roasted garlic over the top. Sprinkle with the rosemary and goat cheese. Place under the broiler until the goat cheese is warm, 45 to 60 seconds. Remove from the oven and drizzle with extra olive oil to serve.

Dinner

Over the years, my perspective on dinner has changed in a major way. Once upon a time, it was a meal I'd eat hastily, as little more than a passing thought. Now, I think of dinner as a luxury, and I look forward to it. It helps me slow down at the end of the day. I'll put on some music, pour myself a glass of wine, and dance around the kitchen as I cook. Then, when my husband gets home, we'll (usually) sit down at the table and chat about the events of the day. Dinnertime is a wonderful ritual: it's such a nice break from the constant stream of to-do lists and emails that characterize chaotic weekdays.

Although I try to make just about everything from scratch when I can, on some rushed weeknights it just isn't possible. On evenings like those, I rely on suitable prepackaged alternatives, such as whole wheat lasagna noodles, corn tortillas, and even fresh pizza dough if I'm really in a pinch. You can go ahead and do the same.

Although I rely on the recipes in chapter 3 for most of my lunches and dinners, some nights simply call for a big, hearty meal, and nothing else will do. That's where these recipes come in; they're the meals I prepare if we're having company, or if I'm planning for leftovers to eat at meals throughout the week. Also, a few of these meals—like the lasagna and enchiladas— make lovely freezer meals. When my friends get pregnant, I make sure their freezers are stocked up with plenty of these dishes in case they don't have time or energy to cook.

< Shredded Carrots, Ginger, and Brown Rice Stuffed Peppers

Pizza

My love of cooking really began when I met my husband. He, being a stereotypical bachelor, lived on fast food and basically ate whatever he felt like—for better or, more often, worse. I couldn't watch him do that to himself, so I started cooking him dinner. I'd enjoyed cooking before, but it wasn't until then that I got serious about learning. One of the very first recipes I learned to make was homemade pizza. I've come a long way since that pizza, of course, but it still makes an appearance in our house at least twice a month.

My family has a long tradition of making homemade pizza, and one of my fondest memories is of standing in my aunt's kitchen, grating cheese for the family pizza dinner we were about to enjoy. My mother's homemade pizza was a staple in our house, too—her version was dotted with fresh herbs for a delicious intensity of flavor. All this is to say that I'm a pizza lover through and through.

If you've ever found your homemade pizza a little lackluster, I highly suggest purchasing a pizza stone. Pizza crust benefits from hotter ovens, and using a pizza stone helps compensate for the fact that most home ovens barely stretch above 500°F (250°C, or gas mark 10). Also, the sauce and cheese matter. I'd use fresh mozzarella all the time if I had my way, but my husband likes a combination of cheeses. Play around with a variety of cheeses, and see what you like best!

Homemade Pizza

YIELD: ONE 14-INCH (35.5 CM) PIZZA, 1½ CUPS (360 G) TOMATO SAUCE

Crust
½ cup (120 ml) warm water
2 tablespoons (40 g) honey
2½ teaspoons active dry yeast
2 tablespoons (30 ml) olive oil
½ teaspoon sea salt
¾ cup (90 g) unbleached all-purpose flour
¾ cup plus 2 tablespoons (104 g) white whole wheat flour, divided
Fine-ground cornmeal, for rolling

Tomato Sauce
1 pound (455 g) Roma tomatoes
½ medium red onion
2 cloves garlic, minced
1 tablespoon (15 ml) olive oil
½ teaspoon sea salt
6 fresh basil leaves
1 tablespoon (15 ml) lemon juice

Topping
2 to 3 cups (320 to 480 g) assorted diced vegetables
3 ounces (84 g) shredded mozzarella cheese
3 ounces (84 g) shredded Cheddar cheese
1 tablespoon (15 ml) olive oil
½ teaspoon garlic powder

To make the crust: In the bowl of a stand mixer fitted with a dough hook (or in a bowl and using a wooden spoon), combine the water, honey, and yeast. Let sit until the yeast activates, 5 to 10 minutes. Stir in the olive oil, sea salt, unbleached all-purpose flour, and ½ cup (60 g) of the white whole wheat flour. Turn on the mixer and mix until the dough comes together, adding 1 tablespoon (7 g) of the white whole wheat flour at a time until the dough begins to pull away from the sides of the bowl and is no longer sticky. Remove from the

Roasted Sweet Potato and Adobo Pizza

mixer, cover with a warm, damp towel, and place the bowl in a draft-free spot to rise for 1 hour.

To make the sauce: Preheat the oven to 425°F (220°C, or gas mark 7). Quarter the Roma tomatoes and onion. Toss with the garlic, olive oil, and salt. Spread in a roasting pan and cook until the tomatoes are tender and lightly charred, 40 to 45 minutes. Place in a food processor along with the basil and lemon juice. Pulse a few times to make sauce; set aside.

After the initial rise, punch down the dough and preheat the oven to 500°F (250°C, or gas mark 10) with a pizza stone, if using. Allow the dough to rise once more while the oven preheats.

Sprinkle the cornmeal on a cutting board or pizza peel. Turn the dough out onto the cornmeal and roll into a 14-inch (35.5 cm) circle (or rectangle, depending on the pizza stone). Spread the sauce evenly over the dough and sprinkle with the diced vegetables and cheeses. Brush the edge of the crust with the olive oil and sprinkle with the garlic powder.

Carefully slide the pizza onto the preheated pizza stone and bake until the crust is browned and the cheese is bubbling, 12 to 15 minutes. Remove from the oven and let cool for 5 minutes before slicing.

 If desired, 100 percent whole wheat flour can be used in place of the unbleached all-purpose flour.

SPRING

Scallion and Spinach

YIELD: ONE 14-INCH (35.5 CM) PIZZA

• •

1 recipe Homemade Pizza Crust (page 114)

Topping
1 bunch scallions
2 cups (80 g) shredded spinach, lightly packed

Sauce
1 cup (240 g) ricotta
1 teaspoon oregano
¼ teaspoon sea salt
¼ teaspoon black pepper

Prepare the Homemade Pizza Crust as directed.

To make the topping: Dice the white parts of the scallions, plus about 1 inch (2.5 cm) of the green parts. Toss with the shredded spinach and set aside.

To make the sauce: In a bowl, stir together the ricotta, oregano, salt, and pepper.

Make the Homemade Pizza as directed, using the ricotta mixture in place of the tomato sauce and the spinach mixture as the topping.

 SUMMER

Charred Corn and Rosemary

YIELD: ONE 14-INCH (35.5 CM) PIZZA

• •

1 recipe Homemade Pizza Crust (page 114)
2 ears sweet corn
2 tablespoons (30 ml) olive oil, divided
2 tablespoons (3 g) rosemary
1 clove garlic, minced
4 ounces (112 g) mozzarella, shredded
2 ounces (56 g) Gorgonzola, crumbled

Prepare the Homemade Pizza Crust as directed. Once the crust is past the first rise, light a grill to medium-low heat.

Shuck the corn and remove any silks still left. Rub the corn with ½ tablespoon (7 ml) of the olive oil and place on the grill. Cook, turning occasionally, until charred, 6 to 8 minutes. Remove from the heat, let cool slightly, then remove the kernels from the cob.

Roll out the crust as directed, and brush the top with ½ tablespoon (7 ml) of the olive oil. Place the crust olive-oil-side down on the grill and cook until puffed and browned. Flip and brush the remaining 1 tablespoon (15 ml) olive oil onto the dough, then sprinkle on the rosemary, garlic, charred corn kernels, and cheeses.

Grill the pizza until the cheese has melted and the crust has a nice char. If the crust is cooking too fast, move the pizza to a cooler part of the grill.

Pear and Blue Cheese

YIELD: ONE 14-INCH (35.5 CM) PIZZA

. . . .

1 recipe Homemade Pizza Crust (page 114)
2 tablespoons (30 ml) olive oil
2 cloves garlic, minced
1 large pear, peeled and thinly sliced
¼ cup (25 g) roasted pecan pieces
4 ounces (112 g) shredded mozzarella cheese
2 ounces (56 g) blue cheese
1 to 2 tablespoons (20 to 40 g) honey, for drizzling

Prepare the Homemade Pizza Crust as directed. When ready to bake, brush the crust with olive oil and sprinkle on the minced garlic. Layer on the thinly sliced pears, sprinkle with the pecans, and finish with the cheeses.

Before serving, drizzle the honey over the baked pizza.

Roasted Sweet Potato and Adobo

YIELD: ONE 14-INCH (35.5 CM) PIZZA

. . . .

1 recipe Homemade Pizza Crust (page 114)
2 cups (280 g) ¼-inch (6 mm) diced sweet potatoes (2 medium)
1 poblano pepper, seeds removed and diced
½ red onion, diced
3 tablespoons (45 ml) adobo sauce
1 chipotle in adobo sauce, minced
1 tablespoon (15 ml) olive oil
1 tablespoon (20 g) honey
1 tablespoon (15 ml) lime juice

Sauce
⅓ cup (80 g) crème fraîche
3 tablespoons (3 g) minced cilantro
1 tablespoon (15 ml) lime juice
¼ teaspoon salt

Prepare the Homemade Pizza Crust as directed.

Preheat the oven to 400°F (200°C, or gas mark 6). In a large bowl, toss the sweet potatoes with the poblano pepper, red onion, adobo sauce, chipotle, olive oil, honey, and lime juice. Roast until tender, 25 to 28 minutes.

To make the sauce: In a small bowl, whisk together the crème fraîche, cilantro, lime juice, and salt.

Continue making the pizza as directed, using the crème fraîche in place of the tomato sauce and the roasted sweet potatoes as the topping.

Homemade Ravioli

Growing up in the rural Midwest, I found that being a vegetarian wasn't the easiest thing in the world. Most restaurants didn't offer any vegetarian options beyond salads, and that often meant my meals out consisted of a nice iceberg lettuce salad with a side of French fries (I've always had a weakness for fries). And when a restaurant did have a vegetarian entrée on the menu, it was nearly always pasta—and at one slightly upscale restaurant my family frequented, that meant frozen ravioli.

And that wasn't necessarily a bad thing. Even though I'm guilty of making snide comments when pasta is the only veggie option at a restaurant, I still turn to it often when I'm cooking at home. This was especially true when my husband—who's not a vegetarian—and I first moved in together. I discovered that ravioli was a dish we could both enjoy, thanks to our mutual love of cheese. Then I'd whip up a big batch and freeze most of it for quick dinners throughout the month.

This ravioli is one of those dishes that might seem intimidating, but don't worry. The end result doesn't have to be pretty. I keep an inexpensive ravioli stamp in my kitchen drawer. It doesn't take up a lot of space and seals the ravioli well. But if pasta making isn't something you want to try, wonton wrappers are great for making quick ravioli. Simply fill one square- or circle-shaped wonton wrapper, brush the edges with water, then top with another wrapper, and cook as you would pasta for 4 to 5 minutes, until tender. Plus, any leftover wrappers can be used to make potstickers (page 80)!

Wholesome Ravioli

YIELD: 20 RAVIOLI, 4 SERVINGS

. . . .

Pasta Dough
1½ cups (180 g) whole wheat pastry flour, plus extra
½ teaspoon sea salt
2 large eggs
2 tablespoons (30 ml) water

Filling
1 cup (240 g) whole-milk ricotta
1 teaspoon minced fresh rosemary
1 teaspoon minced fresh parsley
1 teaspoon minced fresh thyme
2 ounces (54 g) grated Parmesan cheese

Sauce
¼ cup (56 g) unsalted butter
2 tablespoons (30 ml) olive oil
2 shallots, thinly sliced

To make the dough: Combine the flour and sea salt on a clean, flat work surface. Make a well in the middle of the flour mixture and crack the eggs in the center, then add the water. Using a fork, whisk the eggs and water, and then slowly begin to incorporate the flour. Continue to combine the flour and eggs until the dough starts to pull together. Continue mixing, eventually using your hands, until the dough is smooth.

Black Pepper and Scallion Ravioli

To make the filling: In a bowl, combine the ricotta, herbs, and Parmesan cheese.

Divide the dough into 8 pieces, roughly 1½ ounces (40 g) each. Using a rolling pin or pasta maker, roll out into strips that are roughly 2½ to 3 inches (6.4 to 7.5 cm) wide and 13 inches (33 cm) long. Place five 1-tablespoon (15 g) dollops of ricotta filling along the pasta strip, then top with another strip of dough. Using a square ravioli cutter, cut into squares.

Bring a pot of water to a boil and add the ravioli to it, 4 or 5 at a time. Cook until the ravioli float to the top, 5 to 6 minutes. Remove with a slotted spoon and place in a bowl, then cover while you cook the remaining ravioli.

To make the sauce: Melt the butter and olive oil together in a large skillet. Add the shallots and cook until translucent and tender, 6 to 7 minutes. Stir in the ravioli and serve.

 Ravioli can be frozen before cooking. Place in a single layer, between pieces of parchment paper, and freeze.

SPRING

Black Pepper and Scallion

YIELD: 20 RAVIOLI, 4 SERVINGS

. . . .

1 recipe Wholesome Ravioli (page 118)
1 teaspoon black pepper
¼ cup (25 g) minced scallion
1 teaspoon honey

Prepare the ravioli as directed, adding the black pepper to the dry ingredients of the pasta dough. Replace the herbs in the filling with the minced scallion and honey.

 Minced garlic scapes would make a lovely substitution for the scallions.

 SUMMER

Summer Squash with Roasted Tomato Sauce

YIELD: 20 RAVIOLI, 4 SERVINGS

. . . .

1 recipe Wholesome Ravioli (page 118)
1 cup (120 g) ¼-inch (6 mm) cubed summer squash
½ tablespoon olive oil
¼ teaspoon sea salt
¼ teaspoon black pepper
1 tablespoon (2 g) minced basil
1 recipe Tomato Sauce (page 114)

Preheat the oven to 425°F (220°C, or gas mark 7). Toss the summer squash with the olive oil, salt, and pepper, spread on a baking sheet, and roast for 12 to 15 minutes, until tender. Reduce the ricotta in the Homemade Ravioli recipe to ¾ cup (180 g), add the minced basil to it, and continue with the recipe, serving with the tomato sauce instead of the butter and shallot sauce.

FALL

Pumpkin with Crispy Sage

YIELD: 20 RAVIOLI, 4 SERVINGS

· ·

1 recipe Wholesome Ravioli (page 118)
1¼ cups (275 g) pumpkin purée
1 ounce (28 g) Gorgonzola, crumbled
¼ teaspoon sea salt
½ teaspoon black pepper
4 or 5 fresh sage leaves

In a small bowl, stir together the pumpkin purée, crumbled Gorgonzola, sea salt, and black pepper. Make the Homemade Ravioli as directed, using the pumpkin mixture as the filling.

Make the butter sauce as directed but add the sage and cook for 2 to 3 minutes, until the sage is crisp.

To serve, place the ravioli on a platter and pour the butter mixture over the pasta. Lightly toss to combine.

 WINTER

Three Cheese with Leek Cream Sauce

YIELD: 20 RAVIOLI, 4 SERVINGS

· ·

1 recipe Wholesome Ravioli (page 118)
2 ounces (54 g) shredded fontina cheese
2 ounces (54 g) shredded Havarti cheese
½ cup (120 g) ricotta
¼ teaspoon sea salt
¼ teaspoon black pepper

Sauce
1 tablespoon (14 g) unsalted butter
2 leeks, rinsed and sliced
1 cup (240 ml) vegetable broth
½ cup (120 ml) heavy cream
¼ teaspoon salt
⅛ teaspoon pepper

Stir together the shredded cheeses, ricotta, salt, and pepper. Make the Homemade Ravioli as directed, using the cheese mixture as the filling.

To make the sauce: Heat the butter in a skillet, add the leeks, and cook for 2 to 3 minutes, then add the vegetable broth and cook for 4 to 5 minutes. Stir in the heavy cream, salt, and pepper and cook over low heat until slightly thickened, 4 to 5 minutes. Add the cooked ravioli to the leek sauce, tossing to combine.

Tacos

A taco is only as good as its tortilla. I started out my taco-eating life as a flour tortilla lover, and always hated the vaguely rubbery texture of store-bought corn tortillas. But once I started making fresh corn tortillas at home, I was hooked. Don't be fooled into thinking they're difficult: tortillas are not only easy to make at home, they're fun, too. And to make things even easier, cheap tortilla presses that make quick work of homemade tortillas can be found online or in specialty cooking stores.

As for fillings, black beans are my protein of choice, but I've also used lentils or chickpeas. If you're like me and want to add a bit of extra heat to the mix, just sprinkle ½ teaspoon of chipotle powder into the bean mix as it cooks. Finally, I think these tacos are wonderful with the tomato salsa on page 87.

Black Bean Tacos

YIELD: 8 TACOS

Corn Tortillas
1 cup (120 g) masa harina
¼ teaspoon sea salt
¾ to 1 cup (180 to 240 ml) warm water

Filling
1½ cups (390 g) black beans with liquid
1 clove garlic, minced
2 tablespoons (30 ml) lime juice
1 teaspoon cumin powder
1 teaspoon ground coriander

Tacos
1 to 2 tablespoons (15 to 30 ml) olive oil
1 cup (70 g) shredded lettuce (optional)
½ cup (80 g) diced tomatoes (optional)
2 avocados, peeled, pitted, and sliced
½ cup (130 g) salsa, homemade (page 87)
  or store-bought

To make the tortillas: In a bowl, combine the masa harina and sea salt. Pour in ¾ cup (180 ml) of the water and stir until a soft dough forms. The dough should be easily workable, not tough or sticky.

Add more of the remaining ¼ cup (60 ml) water as needed. Cover and let sit for 20 minutes.

Divide the dough into 8 golf ball–size pieces. Flatten with a tortilla press or, alternatively, place on a clean, nonstick surface and press down with the back of a flat bowl or plate. The tortillas should be roughly 6 inches (15 cm) in diameter.

To make the filling: In a small saucepan or skillet, combine the black beans, garlic, lime juice, cumin, and coriander. Cook over medium-low heat for 8 to 10 minutes, until the mixture has thickened and the majority of the liquid has evaporated.

To make the tacos: Brush both sides of the tortilla with olive oil, place in a dry skillet over medium heat, and cook on each side for 20 to 30 seconds, until browning and forming air pockets, then remove and place in a damp towel. Repeat with the remaining tortillas.

Layer on roughly ¼ cup (60 g) of the black beans and top with the lettuce, tomatoes, avocado, and a couple spoonfuls of salsa.

SPRING

Roasted Beets and Sprouts

YIELD: 8 TACOS

. . . .

Beets

3 medium red beets

1 tablespoon (15 ml) olive oil

½ teaspoon salt

½ teaspoon pepper

¼ teaspoon cayenne pepper (or to taste)

1½ cups (390 g) chickpeas, drained and rinsed

2 tablespoons (30 ml) lime juice

2 tablespoons (2 g) minced fresh cilantro

¼ teaspoon sea salt

1 recipe Corn Tortillas (page 122)

½ cup (30 g) sprouts, such as radish, broccoli, or alfalfa

To make the beets: Preheat the oven to 400°F (200°C, or gas mark 6). Wash, peel, and cut the beets into ¼-inch (6 mm) cubes. Toss with the olive oil and seasonings. Bake until tender, 20 to 25 minutes.

Place the chickpeas in a bowl and mash with the back of a fork. Stir in the lime juice, cilantro, and salt. Assemble the tacos by layering the chickpea mixture and the roasted beets on the tortillas and topping with the sprouts.

 SUMMER

Grilled Zucchini with Spicy Sweet Corn Relish

YIELD: 8 TACOS

. . . .

1 recipe Black Bean Tacos (page 122)

1 medium zucchini, trimmed

½ tablespoon (8 ml) olive oil

¼ teaspoon each sea salt and black pepper

Corn Relish

1 medium ear sweet corn, shucked

1 jalapeño pepper

1 tablespoon each (20 g) honey, (15 ml) lime juice, and (1 g) minced cilantro

Preheat a grill to medium. Cut the zucchini in half horizontally. Slice each half lengthwise into ¼-inch (6 mm) thick slices. Toss with the olive oil, salt, and pepper. Grill 2 to 3 minutes per side. Remove from heat and let cool slightly. Cut into thin strips.

To make the corn relish: Place the corn on the grill with the jalapeño, alongside the zucchini. Grill, turning occasionally, 5 to 6 minutes. Remove from the heat and let cool slightly.

Remove the kernels from the cob and mince the jalapeño, removing the seeds if desired. In a small bowl, toss the corn and jalapeño with the honey, lime juice, and cilantro.

Make the Black Beans Tacos as directed and assemble, topping with the grilled zucchini and corn relish.

FALL

Cauliflower Rice

YIELD: 8 TACOS

. . . .

1 recipe Black Bean Tacos (page 122)
½ head cauliflower
2 tablespoons (20 g) minced onion
1 tablespoon (15 ml) freshly squeezed lime juice
¼ cup (4 g) fresh cilantro
¼ teaspoon black pepper
¼ teaspoon sea salt

Steam the cauliflower until it's tender, but still has a bit of crunch, 6 to 7 minutes. Pulse in a food processor along with the onion, lime juice, cilantro, black pepper, and sea salt until the cauliflower mixture resembles rice. Make the Black Bean Tacos as directed, spooning the cauliflower mixture over the bean filling and serve with the avocado slices and salsa, if desired.

 WINTER

Harissa Butternut Squash

YIELD: 6 TO 8 TACOS, 3 TO 4 SERVINGS

. . . .

1 recipe Black Bean Tacos (page 122)

Harissa
1 red bell pepper, roasted (page 77)
1 chipotle in adobo sauce
2 tablespoons (30 ml) adobo sauce
3 tablespoons (3 g) fresh cilantro
1 clove garlic
Juice from ½ lime
2 tablespoons (30 ml) olive oil
½ teaspoon each cumin and coriander
¼ teaspoon sea salt

3 cups (420 g) cubed butternut squash
¼ red onion, roughly chopped

Preheat the oven to 400˚F (200˚C, or gas mark 6).

To make the harissa: Combine all the harissa ingredients in a food processor or blender and process until well combined. Taste and adjust the seasonings as desired.

In a roasting pan, combine the cubed butternut squash, red onion, and harissa; stir until the squash is well coated. Roast the squash until tender and browned, 30 to 35 minutes.

Make the Black Bean Tacos as directed, spooning the roasted butternut squash over the black bean filling.

Stuffed Peppers

My husband is willing to try just about anything when it comes to my cooking, but there are still a couple of meals he avoids, having been traumatized by them in his childhood. For instance, I rave up and down about tamales, but he's yet to try any batch I've made. And working stuffed peppers into our meal rotation has been slow going, to say the least. That's because he has distant memories of bland beef- and rice-stuffed green peppers, and, for the longest time, equated that blindingly awful experience with any stuffed pepper I'd put on his plate. That is, until I left a stuffed pepper sitting innocently on the counter. Without asking questions, he tried a bite, and then mentioned casually that he liked "whatever that was." Ever since, he's been a bit more open to the idea, and I've enjoyed finding new flavors to pair with the pepper stuffing.

Another reason I really love this stuffed pepper recipe is because I am notorious for having small amounts of leftover cooked grains and beans stashed in my refrigerator. Stuffing a pepper with these leftovers adds healthy bulk to the meal. The seasonal variations here are ones I enjoy, but if I'm being honest, I could toss any combination of grains and beans into a pepper and live happily ever after.

I specify red or green peppers in these recipes but any sizable pepper would work fine. If you can find them, Hatch chiles are amazing, and poblanos make a good runner-up. Whatever you do, use a milder chile, and watch out for seeds. If you like your peppers on the firm side, skip the broiling and stuff them raw. You can also stuff the peppers a day or two ahead of time, making for a quick dinner (or dinners) during the week.

Simple Stuffed Peppers

YIELD: 2 TO 4 SERVINGS

2 green or red bell peppers
¾ cup (120 g) cooked grains
½ cup (130 g) beans, drained and rinsed
2 ounces (56 g) shredded cheese
½ teaspoon sea salt
¼ teaspoon black pepper

Turn on your oven's broiler or preheat your oven to 500°F (250°C, or gas mark 10). Broil the peppers, turning occasionally, until soft and starting to blister, 1 to 2 minutes. Let cool slightly. Place in a roasting pan and cut a slit down the side of each pepper. Remove the core and seeds. Lower the oven temperature to 375°F (190°C, or gas mark 5).

In a bowl, combine the cooked grains, beans, shredded cheese, salt, and black pepper. Stuff the peppers with the grain mixture and place in a baking dish. Bake until the cheese is melted and the filling is hot, 20 to 25 minutes.

SPRING

Cheesy Broccoli and Barley

YIELD: 2 TO 4 SERVINGS

. . . .

2 green or red bell peppers
2 cups (120 g) raw broccoli florets
½ cup (130 g) white beans or chickpeas, drained and rinsed
¼ teaspoon salt
¼ teaspoon pepper
½ teaspoon garlic powder
¼ teaspoon smoked paprika
3 ounces (84 g) shredded Cheddar cheese, divided
½ cup (76 g) cooked barley

Prepare the Simple Stuffed Peppers as directed (page 125).

In a pot of boiling water, blanch the broccoli until bright green, 2 minutes. Pulse the beans, salt, pepper, garlic powder, and smoked paprika in a food processor until slightly broken down. Add the broccoli and 1 cup (120 g) of the cheese, pulsing again until just combined. Stir in the barley. Fill the peppers with the mixture and place in a baking dish. Top the peppers with the remaining ½ cup (60 g) Cheddar cheese.

Bake the peppers until the cheese is melted and the filling is hot, 20 to 25 minutes.

 Cauliflower makes a great substitute for the broccoli.

 SUMMER

"Lasagna" Stuffed Peppers

YIELD: 2 TO 4 SERVINGS

. . . .

2 green or red bell peppers
2 ounces (56 g) whole wheat orzo
½ cup (120 g) whole-milk ricotta
1 egg white
½ teaspoon dried oregano
¼ teaspoon sea salt
¼ teaspoon black pepper
¾ cup (190 g) tomato sauce (page 114)
2 ounces (56 g) shredded mozzarella cheese

Prepare the Simple Stuffed Peppers as directed (page 125). Cook the orzo, drain, and set aside. Stir together the ricotta, egg white, oregano, salt, and pepper.

Slice the peppers in half and layer with the tomato sauce, orzo, ricotta, and then more tomato sauce. Sprinkle the peppers with the shredded mozzarella cheese. Place in a baking dish.

Bake the peppers until the cheese is melted and the filling is hot, 20 to 25 minutes.

FALL

Shredded Carrots, Ginger, and Brown Rice

YIELD: 2 TO 4 SERVINGS

. . . .

2 green or red bell peppers
1 cup (200 g) cooked brown rice
1 cup (80 g) shredded carrot
2 teaspoons minced ginger
2 tablespoons (30 ml) soy sauce
2 tablespoons (2 g) minced cilantro
1 tablespoon (15 ml) tahini

Prepare the Simple Stuffed Peppers as directed (page 125). Combine the brown rice with the shredded carrot, ginger, soy sauce, cilantro, and tahini. Fill the peppers with the mixture and place in a baking dish. Bake the peppers until the filling is hot, 20 to 25 minutes.

 WINTER

Quinoa with Parsnip Purée

YIELD: 2 TO 4 SERVINGS

. . . .

2 green or red bell peppers
1 medium parsnip, cubed
2 tablespoons (30 ml) lemon juice
2 teaspoons lemon zest
1 tablespoon (1 g) minced dill
3 tablespoons (45 g) plain whole-milk Greek-style yogurt
½ cup (70 g) cooked quinoa

Prepare the Simple Stuffed Peppers as directed (page 125). Boil the parsnip until tender, 4 to 5 minutes. Drain and purée with the lemon juice, zest, dill, and Greek yogurt. Stir in the cooked quinoa. Fill the peppers with the mixture and place in a baking dish. Bake the peppers until the filling is hot, 20 to 25 minutes.

Lasagna

When I was younger, I came to a rather stark realization about lasagna. I was at a friend's house and was invited to stay for dinner. Of course I said yes, and when dinner was served, I was over the moon. It was lasagna with a side of garlic bread! I dug in happily—and then, a flash of panic washed over me. There was something unusual in the lasagna: meat. For years, I believed that "lasagna" meant noodles, ricotta cheese, and some form of pasta sauce, and that it was vegetarian by definition. (It wasn't that my family was vegetarian: we simply never had meat in our pasta sauce.)

To this day, I'm still a steadfast lover of vegetarian lasagna. This dish is one of those "perfect for all occasions" recipes. I've made it when we're having company over; on days when I want a solid week of leftovers to put in my husband's packed lunch; and for my pregnant friends as a freezer meal for future use. (It's a great gift!) I keep the layers fairly simple, and I try not to overdo it on the cheese. Lasagna is all about striking a balance between sauce, noodles, and filling.

When time permits I like to make lasagna from scratch—noodles, sauce, and all. Of course, that's not always doable, and that's when store-bought supplies come in handy.

Vegetable-Laden Lasagna

YIELD: 9 SERVINGS

. . . .

Noodles
1½ cups (180 g) whole wheat pastry flour
½ teaspoon salt
2 large eggs
2 tablespoons (30 ml) water

Filling
1 tablespoon (15 ml) olive oil
1 medium onion, diced
4 to 5 cups (640 to 800 g) cubed assorted
  vegetables

Ricotta
One 15-ounce (420 g) container ricotta
1 large egg white
1 tablespoon (2 g) oregano
½ teaspoon salt
3 cups (780 g) tomato sauce (page 114, recipe
  doubled) or béchamel sauce (recipe follows)
4 to 6 ounces (112 to 168 g) shredded
  mozzarella cheese (if using tomato sauce)

**Béchamel Sauce
(optional, instead of tomato sauce)**
2 tablespoons (28 g) butter
1 small shallot
3 tablespoons (24 g) flour
2 cups (480 ml) whole milk
6 ounces (168 g) shredded mozzarella cheese,
  divided

To make the noodles: Combine the whole wheat flour and salt on a clean work surface. Make a well in the center, crack in the eggs, and add the water. Using a fork, whisk the eggs and slowly begin to incorporate flour into the mixture. Continue to do this, and a paste will soon form. Continue to mix (eventually ditching the fork, and using your hands instead), and knead the dough into a smooth ball. Let sit for 20 to 30 minutes.

Preheat the oven to 400°F (200°C, or gas mark 6).

To make the filling: While the pasta dough sits, toss together the olive oil, diced onion, and veggies. Spread in a roasting pan and roast until tender, 25 to 35 minutes (depending on the vegetables; check every 5 minutes after 25 minutes).

Divide the pasta dough into 9 even pieces. Using a pasta attachment or rolling pin, roll out the pasta into lasagna noodles. The pasta should be thin, but should still hold together.

To make the ricotta: Whisk together the ricotta, egg white, oregano, and salt.

Bring a pot of water to a boil. Working in batches, boil the noodles as you assemble the lasagna. Pour ½ cup (130 g) of the tomato sauce in the bottom of a 9 by 9-inch (23 by 23 cm) pan. Boil 3 pasta noodles for 30 seconds and layer in the pan. Smear half the ricotta cheese mixture on the noodles, sprinkle half the veggies on top, and then top with roughly one-third of the shredded cheese.

Repeat the process again with tomato sauce, noodles (boiled for 30 seconds), the second half of the ricotta mixture, the second half of the vegetable mixture, and another one-third of the cheese. To finish, spread another ½ cup (130 g) of tomato sauce, boil the remaining 3 noodles, and layer them on top, then cover with more tomato sauce and the remaining one-third cheese. Bake for 30 to 35 minutes, until the cheese is golden brown and the tomato sauce is bubbling.

If you prefer béchamel: Melt the butter in a saucepan over medium-low heat. Add the minced shallot and cook until fragrant and translucent, 5 to 6 minutes. Whisk in the flour and cook for another minute. Stir in the milk and heat until the béchamel has thickened, 4 to 6 minutes. Remove from the heat and stir in 4 ounces (112 g) of the cheese until melted. Use the béchamel as you would tomato sauce, sprinkling the remaining 2 ounces (56 g) of cheese on top of the lasagna.

SPRING

Fennel and Spinach

YIELD: 9 SERVINGS

. . . .

1 recipe Vegetable-Laden Lasagna (page 128)
1 tablespoon (15 ml) olive oil
1 head fennel, thinly sliced
3 cups (120 g) packed spinach

Heat the olive oil over medium-low heat. Add the fennel and cook for 6 to 8 minutes until tender. Remove from the heat and stir in the spinach.

Prepare the Vegetable-Laden Lasagna as directed, using the béchamel sauce instead of the tomato sauce and the fennel and spinach mixture as the filling.

 SUMMER

Grilled Zucchini

YIELD: 9 SERVINGS

. . . .

1 recipe Vegetable-Laden Lasagna (page 128)
12 ounces (340 g) zucchini (2 medium)

Preheat the grill to medium-low heat.

Cut the ends off the zucchini and cut in half horizontally. Take each half and slice into ¼-inch (6 mm) thick strips. Grill until the zucchini is lightly charred, 2 to 3 minutes per side. Remove from the grill and cut into small pieces.

Make the Vegetable-Laden Lasagna as directed, using the tomato sauce and the grilled zucchini as the filling.

 To make this meal even healthier, leave the zucchini in long strips instead of chopping it up, and use it to replace the whole wheat noodles.

< *Grilled Zucchini Lasagna*

FALL

Roasted Apple and Butternut Squash

YIELD: 9 SERVINGS

. . . .

1 recipe Vegetable-Laden Lasagna (page 128)
3 cups (420 g) cubed butternut squash
1 medium apple, peeled and cubed
1 tablespoon (15 ml) olive oil

Preheat the oven to 425˚F (220˚C, or gas mark 7). Toss the butternut squash and apple with the olive oil and spread out in a roasting pan. Bake for 25 minutes. Reduce the oven to 400˚F (200˚C, or gas mark 6) and continue with the Vegetable-Laden Lasagna as directed, using the béchamel sauce.

 WINTER

Sweet Potato Purée

YIELD: 9 SERVINGS

. . . .

1 recipe Vegetable-Laden Lasagna (page 128)
1 large sweet potato, cubed
1 cup (235 ml) milk

Peel and cube the sweet potato. Bring a large pot of water to a boil, add the sweet potato, and cook until tender, 12 to 15 minutes. Drain and purée with the milk. Continue with Vegetable-Laden Lasagna recipe as directed, using the sweet potato purée in place of milk in the béchamel sauce and leaving out the vegetables.

Burgers

I try not to be a huge food snob. I like strong flavors and fresh meals, and I'll try anything once. However, when it comes to a good vegetarian burger, I have very specific criteria. After it's grilled, it *must* be slightly crisp on the outside and moist on the inside. And, because I've had my fair share of mushy, unappealing vegetable burgers in my time, I prefer to make my own whenever possible. (I'm also that person who shows up at a cookout with a batch of these burgers. That way, I know I'll have dinner for myself plus plenty to share.)

There are a few different variations of vegetable burgers in my repertoire, and the version I make on any given day depends on the ingredients I have on hand (and on my mood, of course!). I usually alternate between a grain-and-nut-based burger and this bean burger. As far as I'm concerned, this burger is the Holy Grail of veggie burgers: it meets my strict criteria and it won't fall apart when you attempt to eat it. Plus, you don't have to douse it in condiments to make it flavorful. Using spices, such as smoked paprika and oregano, will see to that. As usual, experiment according to your own taste and know that just about any spice combination will work.

These burgers are a bit wet before they're cooked, so wet your hands before trying to shape them into patties. Also, baking these burgers before grilling them helps pull them together. That's a good thing, especially if you plan to grill outside. I also keep a grill pan handy for those days when I want a burger but don't want the fuss of lighting the grill.

Veggie Burgers

YIELD: 4 BURGERS

· ·

¼ onion, diced
½ cup (130 g) chickpeas (drained and rinsed, if using canned)
½ cup (30 g) whole wheat bread crumbs
¼ cup (30 g) whole wheat pastry flour
1 large egg
2 tablespoons (14 g) sunflower seeds
1 tablespoon (15 ml) olive oil
1 tablespoon (15 ml) soy sauce
1 teaspoon oregano
1 teaspoon smoked paprika
¼ teaspoon sea salt
1 cup (40 g) spinach, packed

In a food processor, pulse the onion into small pieces. Add the chickpeas, bread crumbs, flour, egg, sunflower seeds, oil, soy sauce, oregano, paprika, and sea salt, and pulse until the chickpeas are well combined with the flour and egg. Add the spinach and pulse again, just until the spinach is combined with the mixture.

Wet your hands and divide the mixture into 4 parts, then pat into 4 patties. For cooking indoors, add the burgers directly to a preheated grill pan and cook for 8 to 10 minutes, flipping once. Alternatively, bake at 350°F (180°C, or gas mark 4) for 10 minutes, then transfer to a grill and cook for 2 to 3 minutes on each side.

To freeze, bake the burgers, let cool, and freeze until ready to use.

SPRING

Fava Bean with Radish Slaw

YIELD: 4 BURGERS

. . . .

1 recipe Veggie Burgers (page 133)
½ cup (70 g) fava beans, shells and outer skins removed
(page 74)

Radish Slaw
1 cup (120 g) thinly sliced radishes
2 tablespoons (12 g) diced scallion
2 tablespoons (30 ml) apple cider vinegar
1 tablespoon (15 ml) olive oil
1 teaspoon honey
¼ teaspoon sea salt
¼ teaspoon black pepper

Prepare the Veggie Burgers as directed, using the fava beans in place of the chickpeas and leaving out the smoked paprika.

To make the slaw: Combine all the ingredients in a bowl and let sit for at least 30 minutes. Top the cooked burger with the slaw and serve.

 SUMMER

Southwest Black Bean with Salsa

YIELD: 4 BURGERS

. . . .

1 recipe Veggie Burgers (page 133)
¾ cup (75 g) old-fashioned rolled oats
½ cup (130 g) black beans
1 tablespoon (6 g) adobo seasoning (page 62)
1 cup (70 g) kale, packed
1 recipe Radish-Scallion Salsa (page 89)

Pulse the oats in a food processor until they resemble coarse meal, then make the Veggie Burgers as directed, using the black beans in place of the chickpeas, the adobo seasoning in place of the oregano and smoked paprika, the kale instead of the spinach, and omitting the pastry flour and bread crumbs. Serve the burgers with 1 to 2 tablespoons (15 to 30 g) salsa on top.

FALL

Curried Sesame with Avocado

YIELD: 4 BURGERS

. . . .

1 recipe Veggie Burgers (page 133)
1 tablespoon (6 g) curry powder
2 tablespoons (16 g) sesame seeds
½ cup (70 g) cooked quinoa
1 ripe avocado, peeled, pitted, and sliced

Prepare the Veggie Burgers as directed but use the curry powder in place of the spices, the sesame seeds instead of the sunflower seeds, omit the spinach, and add the cooked quinoa. Serve the burgers topped with a few slices of avocado.

 WINTER

Sweet Potato and Lentil

YIELD: 4 BURGERS

. . . .

1 recipe Veggie Burgers (page 133)
½ cup (60 g) cubed sweet potato
1 teaspoon olive oil
½ cup (80 g) black lentils

Preheat the oven to 400°F (200°C, or gas mark 6). Toss the sweet potatoes with the olive oil. Spread out on a baking tray and cook until tender, about 30 minutes.

Bring a small pot of water to a boil and add the black lentils. Cook until the lentils are tender but not mushy, 20 to 22 minutes. Prepare the Veggie Burgers as directed, using the lentils in place of the chickpeas and the sweet potatoes in place of the spinach.

Mac and Cheese

My philosophy when it comes to food? Everything in moderation. I'm not one to pass up a good slice of cake—but I don't eat cake every day, either. That's my attitude toward certain meals, too, such as macaroni and cheese. As a child, I remember watching my mother make it. I'd always sneak into the kitchen and grab a cheese cube or two before they made their way into the pasta. Though I use a different recipe than my mother did, I still have a close emotional connection with mac and cheese, even though I know this dish isn't an everyday (or, really, even an every-week) meal. I save it for when I crave something warm and comforting.

I've made macaroni and cheese many different ways, but somehow I always end up back at this recipe. Making the béchamel sauce takes a few extra steps, but I think the end result is perfectly creamy. The cheese itself also makes a difference to the finished dish, and can take your mac and cheese from so-so to out of this world. Be sure to buy a block of sharp Cheddar and grate it yourself, because many preshredded cheeses have extra ingredients that can affect the consistency of the béchamel sauce.

As for the pasta, I've made my own macaroni with the help of an attachment to my stand mixer, but to be honest, I'm more likely to pick up a box of whole wheat pasta from the store. I usually use shells, but elbow macaroni or fusilli pasta both work just as well. Finally, I prefer whole milk in this recipe, but if you want to use a lower fat milk, go ahead—happily, it won't make too much difference to the mac and cheese's creamy texture.

Creamy Mac and Cheese

YIELD: 3 TO 4 SERVINGS

. . . .

6 ounces (168 g) whole wheat pasta shells
2 tablespoons (28 g) unsalted butter
½ medium yellow onion, diced
½ teaspoon sea salt
¼ teaspoon black pepper
2 tablespoons (16 g) unbleached all-purpose flour
1½ cups (355 ml) whole milk
6 ounces (168 g) Cheddar cheese, grated, divided

Preheat the oven to 375˚F (190˚C, or gas mark 5). Bring a pot of water to a boil. Add the pasta and cook until just tender, 7 to 8 minutes. Drain and set aside.

In a saucepan, melt the butter and add the onion, salt, and pepper. Cook until the onions are translucent, 7 to 8 minutes. Add the flour and cook for another minute. Stir in the milk and heat until thickened, 5 to 6 minutes. Remove from the heat and add half the cheese.

In a 9 by 9-inch (23 by 23 cm) baking dish (or its equivalent), combine the pasta with the cheese sauce and top with the remaining half of the cheese. Bake for 35 to 40 minutes, until the cheese is bubbling and golden brown on top.

 Mac and cheese can be prepared up to a day or two ahead of time and refrigerated until you're ready to serve it.

Spinach and Gouda Mac and Cheese >

SPRING

Spinach and Gouda

YIELD: 3 TO 4 SERVINGS

. . . .

1 recipe Mac and Cheese (page 136)
2 tablespoons (20 g) minced garlic scapes
4 ounces (112 g) smoked Gouda, shredded
2 ounces (56 g) mozzarella, shredded
2 cups (80 g) packed, shredded spinach

Prepare the Mac and Cheese as directed, using the garlic scapes in place of the onion and the Gouda and mozzarella in place of the Cheddar. Add the shredded spinach in with the pasta and cheese before baking, stirring until slightly wilted.

 SUMMER

Sweet Corn and Pepper

YIELD: 3 TO 4 SERVINGS

. . . .

1 recipe Mac and Cheese (page 136)
2 ears sweet corn, kernels removed (roughly 2 cups, or 300 g)
½ red bell pepper, seeded and minced
½ tablespoon olive oil
¼ teaspoon sea salt
½ teaspoon smoked paprika

Preheat the oven to 375°F (190°C, or gas mark 5). In a bowl, combine the sweet corn, minced pepper, olive oil, salt, and smoked paprika, and place in a roasting pan. Roast until the corn is tender, 20 to 25 minutes. Make the Mac and Cheese as directed, stirring the corn in with the pasta and cheese sauce before baking.

FALL

Sweet Potato and Rosemary

YIELD: 3 TO 4 SERVINGS

. . . .

1 recipe Mac and Cheese (page 136)
1 medium sweet potato, peeled and cubed
2 teaspoons rosemary
3 ounces (84 g) Havarti cheese

Bring a pot of water to a boil, add the sweet potato, and cook until soft, 8 to 10 minutes. Drain and transfer to a bowl. Mash and add ¼ cup (60 ml) of the milk from the original recipe and the rosemary to smooth them out. Make the Mac and Cheese as directed, adding the mashed sweet potato with the remaining 1¼ cups (295 ml) milk and adding the Havarti in place of half the Cheddar cheese.

 WINTER

Mushroom and Onion

YIELD: 3 TO 4 SERVINGS

. . . .

1 recipe Mac and Cheese (page 136)
1 tablespoon (15 ml) olive oil
½ cup (70 g) diced red onion
4 ounces (112 g) cremini mushrooms, thinly sliced
3 ounces (84 g) Gouda cheese
3 ounces (84 g) Havarti cheese

In a skillet, heat the olive oil, and cook the onion for 6 to 7 minutes. Add the mushrooms and cook for another 4 to 5 minutes, until soft. Prepare the Mac and Cheese as directed, leaving out the onions and adding the mushroom and onion mixture to the pasta and cheese mixture before baking.

Risotto

I like to get creative in the kitchen by recreating dishes I've eaten elsewhere, like a cookie recipe based on a batch made by a friend, or an entrée I ordered at a restaurant and couldn't get enough of. My process goes something like this: first, if I can, I sample the dish a few times, figuring out exactly what it is I like about it and why. Then I make a few notes, and, finally, when I feel confident, I whip up my own version. Sometimes the result is spot-on. Other times, my version is different from the original, but still really good.

This risotto falls into the latter category. I had made risotto before, but wanted to nail a flavor combination I'd just had in a restaurant. I searched my cupboards high and low for Arborio rice, but, much to my dismay, I didn't have any. But I did have another grain on hand: farro. Farro falls into the "ancient wheat" category, and has a smooth, nutty taste. When it cooks up, it's still slightly chewy—the perfect substitute for Arborio rice! One dish later, I had fallen in love with the farro variation, and it's now my primary risotto recipe.

Risotto may look intimidating, but it isn't. It's really all about having patience. It involves plenty of stirring and some standing around and waiting, though, so I find myself cleaning up parts of the kitchen or reading the newspaper while I make it. Like its traditional counterpart, this farro risotto isn't the same in its leftover form, but I think it's still great when it's reheated with a little extra liquid.

Farro Risotto

YIELD: 2 SERVINGS

· ·

2 cups (480 ml) low-sodium vegetable broth
2 cups (480 ml) water
1 tablespoon (15 ml) olive oil
1 tablespoon (14 g) unsalted butter
1 shallot, minced
¾ cup (140 g) uncooked pearled farro
¼ cup (60 ml) white wine
2 tablespoons (3 g) minced fresh rosemary
⅛ teaspoon salt
2 ounces (56 g) goat cheese (or Gorgonzola, cream cheese, or another creamy cheese)

In a stockpot, bring the vegetable broth and water to a boil, then reduce to a simmer.

In a large skillet with high sides, heat the olive oil and butter over medium-low heat. Add the shallot and sauté until translucent and fragrant. Stir in the farro and toast for 1 minute.

Keeping the heat at medium-low, add the wine and let cook until almost evaporated. Add ½ cup (120 ml) of the hot stock/water mixture. Stir until the farro absorbs the stock. Continue to add more stock, ½ cup (120 ml) at a time, as the farro absorbs it. Do this until the farro is tender, about 45 minutes. Test the farro for tenderness occasionally. When the farro is tender, stir in the rosemary and salt. Cook for 1 to 2 more minutes, then remove from the heat and add the goat cheese. Serve immediately.

Leek and Pear Risotto >

SPRING

Swiss Chard

YIELD: 2 SERVINGS

. . . .

1 recipe Farro Risotto (page 140)
2 tablespoons (20 g) minced green garlic
2 cups (80 g) Swiss chard, stemmed and shredded

Make the Farro Risotto as directed, using the minced green garlic in place of the shallot. Add the chard in with the rosemary, and cook until the liquid has been absorbed, the risotto is tender, and the chard is wilted.

 SUMMER

Shaved Zucchini and Pesto

YIELD: 2 SERVINGS

. . . .

Pesto
2 cloves garlic
1½ cups (60 g) packed basil leaves
⅓ cup (33 g) Parmesan cheese
2 tablespoons (18 g) toasted pine nuts
¼ cup (60 ml) olive oil
3 tablespoons (45 ml) freshly squeezed lemon juice

1 recipe Farro Risotto (page 140)
1 cup (120 g) shredded zucchini

To make the pesto: Purée the pesto ingredients in a food processor or blender until a sauce forms, adding more olive oil or a splash of water to thin it out if necessary.

Make the Farro Risotto as directed, omitting the rosemary and goat cheese and adding ¼ cup (60 g) of the pesto and the shredded zucchini to the risotto toward the end of cooking.

 FALL

Puréed Butternut Squash and Gorgonzola

YIELD: 2 SERVINGS

. . . .

1 recipe Farro Risotto (page 140)
2 cups (280 g) cubed butternut squash
1 tablespoon (14 g) unsalted butter
1 teaspoon thyme
½ teaspoon sea salt
¼ teaspoon black pepper
2 ounces (56 g) Gorgonzola
¼ cup (25 g) crushed pecans
Honey, for drizzling

Bring a pot of water to a boil. Add the cubed butternut squash and cook until soft, 10 to 12 minutes. Drain, transfer to a bowl, and add the butter, thyme, sea salt, and black pepper. Mash until combined.

Make the Farro Risotto as directed, adding the mashed butternut squash at the end along with the Gorgonzola and pecans. Serve with a drizzle of honey.

 WINTER

Leek and Pear

YIELD: 2 SERVINGS

. . . .

1 recipe Farro Risotto (page 140)
2 leeks, sliced, white parts only
1 large pear, peeled and cubed
1 tablespoon (2 g) minced fresh dill, plus extra for serving
3 tablespoons (18 g) mascarpone cheese

Make the Farro Risotto as directed, using the sliced leeks in place of the shallots. Once the farro has fully cooked and the majority of the liquid has been absorbed, stir in the cubed pear, dill, and mascarpone cheese. Serve sprinkled with extra dill.

Savory Galette

My husband and I have different eating habits, especially when it comes to carbs. He could happily give up bread or pastry without missing it, while I wouldn't last a week before being struck with longing for a slice of bread smeared with peanut butter. What's more, I love flaky pastries passionately—croissants, Danishes—anything with a crust, really. And that's where this galette comes into the picture.

This freeform pastry is half about the crust, and half about the filling, and it's one of the few recipes in which I use unbleached all-purpose flour to ensure a wonderfully flaky crust—one that also provides a solid base for just about any filling you can think of.

As for the filling, you could, technically, omit the ricotta and use only vegetables, but I love the ricotta-vegetable layer. And, for the most part, I like to keep the flavors of the filling fairly simple, with hardly anything more than a tablespoon of fresh mixed herbs. A slice of galette and a good side salad make for an elegant dinner that's filling without being overly heavy.

Ricotta Galette

YIELD: 4 TO 6 SERVINGS

Crust

1 cup (120 g) unbleached all-purpose flour or whole wheat pastry flour
¼ teaspoon sea salt
¼ cup (56 g) cold unsalted butter
1 ounce (28 g) cream cheese
1 tablespoon (15 ml) maple syrup
2 tablespoons (30 ml) cold water

Filling

½ cup (120 g) ricotta
2 teaspoons honey
¼ teaspoon black pepper
¼ teaspoon sea salt
1½ cups (240 g) thinly sliced vegetables

2 tablespoons (30 ml) heavy cream
1 large egg

Preheat the oven to 375°F (190°C, or gas mark 5) and cover a baking tray with parchment paper.

To make the crust: In a food processor or large bowl, combine the flour and salt. Cut in the butter and cream cheese, pulsing in a food processor or using your fingers until the dough is in pea-size pieces. Add the maple syrup and water, pulsing or stirring until the dough comes together. Turn out onto a floured work surface and roll the dough into a 10-inch (25 cm) circle. Transfer to the baking tray.

To make the filling: In a bowl, whip together the ricotta, honey, black pepper, and sea salt. Spread the ricotta over the crust, leaving an edge of roughly 1½ inches (3.8 cm). Layer on the vegetables, and fold the edges of the crust over the outer edges of the layered ricotta and vegetables, pleating the crust as you go in order to make an even circle.

Whisk together the heavy cream and egg, then brush the crust with the egg wash. Bake for 40 to 45 minutes, until the crust is golden and the filling is set and bubbling. Remove from the oven and let cool before serving. Store leftovers in an airtight container in the refrigerator for 3 to 4 days.

SPRING

Herbed Red Potato

YIELD: 4 TO 6 SERVINGS

- -

1 recipe Ricotta Galette (page 143)
½ pound (225 g) red potatoes, thinly sliced (⅛ inch, or 3 mm)
1 tablespoon (15 ml) olive oil
2 teaspoons herbes de Provence
¼ teaspoon sea salt (use only if herbes de Provence is salt-free)

Toss the red potatoes with the olive oil, herbes de Provence, and salt. Make the Ricotta Galette as directed, layering the potatoes over the ricotta before baking.

 In this recipe, the potatoes stay a bit on the firm side. If you prefer softer potatoes, boil them for 3 to 4 minutes, just until tender. Let cool, then slice and use in the galette.

 SUMMER

Spiced Eggplant and Feta

YIELD: 4 TO 6 SERVINGS

- -

1 recipe Ricotta Galette (page 143)
2 ounces (56 g) feta cheese, divided
1 small eggplant, cut into ¼-inch (6 mm) slices
1 tablespoon (15 ml) olive oil
2 teaspoons smoked paprika
Pinch of saffron
¼ teaspoon sea salt

Prepare the Ricotta Galette as directed, adding 1 ounce (28 g) of the feta to the ricotta mixture. In a bowl, combine the eggplant, olive oil, smoked paprika, saffron, sea salt, and the remaining 1 ounce (28 g) of feta. Layer the eggplant mixture over the ricotta, and bake as directed.

 FALL

Acorn Squash and Blue Cheese

YIELD: 4 TO 6 SERVINGS

- -

1 recipe Ricotta Galette (page 143)
1 acorn squash
½ cup (120 g) ricotta
1 large egg
1 tablespoon (20 g) honey
½ teaspoon salt
½ teaspoon pepper
2 teaspoons minced fresh sage
2 ounces (56 g) blue cheese

Preheat the oven to 425˚F (220˚C, or gas mark 7). Cut the acorn squash in half and place cut-side down in a roasting dish. Fill the dish with ¼ inch (6 mm) of water and bake the squash until tender, 45 to 55 minutes. Measure out 1 cup (225 g) roasted squash. Save the rest for another use.

In a small bowl, stir together the 1 cup (225 g) of squash, the ricotta, egg, honey, salt, pepper, sage, and blue cheese. Prepare the Ricotta Galette as directed, using the squash mixture in place of the ricotta and vegetable filling. Bake as directed.

 WINTER

Parsnip and Thyme

YIELD: 4 TO 6 SERVINGS

- -

1 recipe Ricotta Galette (page 143)
1 parsnip, thinly shaved
1 tablespoon (14 g) unsalted butter, melted
½ teaspoon dried thyme

Toss the shaved parsnip with the melted butter and thyme. Prepare the Ricotta Galette as directed, layering the parsnip mixture on the ricotta in place of the vegetable filling. Bake as directed.

Parsnip and Thyme Galette >

Enchiladas

If I'd given more foods a chance as a child, I wouldn't be making up for lost time now. My parents loved enchiladas, but I'd look on with disgust every time they'd order them at a restaurant. I usually stuck with what was probably a pretty bland sandwich and fries. I made the mistake of judging enchiladas on looks alone, which led to nearly a decade-long aversion to them.

I can't remember the first time I finally gave in and tried them, but I remember the feeling of delighted shock that kicked in as I realized how perfectly the flavor of the filling melded with the corn tortillas and sauce. Soon, I found myself adding enchiladas to my Ultimate Comfort Food list. Even better, I found that making enchiladas at home is simple, and that it's really easy to get creative with the fillings and sauce.

The filling for my enchiladas is always in flux. It depends completely on seasonal produce. But the sauce is the constant in this equation. It never changes. In fact, during the summer months, I'll can a couple of batches of strained tomatoes for the sole purpose of making enchilada sauce. (Of course, you can also buy strained tomatoes at the supermarket, which makes this sauce quick and fairly easy.) If you like a bit of extra spice, try adding a little cayenne or extra chipotle powder to the sauce, or if you happen to have chipotles in adobo sauce handy, you can use a chipotle and some sauce in place of the chipotle powder.

Black Bean Enchiladas

YIELD: 8 ENCHILADAS

Sauce
1 tablespoon (15 ml) olive oil
½ medium red onion, diced
1 fresh jalapeño, seeded and minced
2 cups (360 g) strained tomatoes
¼ cup (4 g) chopped cilantro
½ teaspoon sea salt
2 tablespoons (30 ml) freshly squeezed
   lime juice
½ teaspoon chipotle powder

Filling
½ cup (125 g) black beans, drained and rinsed
1½ cups (240 g) cooked vegetables

4 ounces (112 g) shredded queso fresco or mild
   white cheese
1 recipe Corn Tortillas (page 122)

Preheat the oven to 375°F (190°C, or gas mark 5).

To make the sauce: In a medium saucepan, heat the olive oil over medium-low heat. Stir in the diced onion and jalapeño and cook for 7 to 8 minutes, until the onions are translucent. Add the tomatoes, cilantro, salt, lime juice, and chipotle powder. Bring to a boil, reduce to a simmer, and cook for 5 minutes.

To make the filling: In a bowl, toss the black beans with the vegetables.

Place half the sauce in the bottom of a 9 by 9-inch (23 by 23 cm) pan. Fill each tortilla with roughly ¼ cup (60 g) of the filling, and place seam-side down in the pan. Top with the remaining half of the sauce and sprinkle with the cheese. Bake for 30 to 35 minutes, until the sauce is bubbling and the cheese is golden brown.

Roasted Vegetable Enchiladas >

SPRING

Collard and Garlic Scapes

YIELD: 8 ENCHILADAS

· ·

1 recipe Black Bean Enchiladas (page 146)
1 cup (40 g) packed shredded collard greens
¼ cup (40 g) minced garlic scapes

Make the Black Bean Enchiladas as directed, tossing the shredded collards and garlic scapes with the black beans.

 SUMMER

Roasted Vegetable

YIELD: 8 ENCHILADAS

· ·

1 recipe Black Bean Enchiladas (page 146)
1 cup (120 g) diced zucchini
½ cup (75 g) diced red pepper
¼ cup (35 g) diced red onion
½ tablespoon olive oil
⅛ teaspoon sea salt

Preheat the oven to 400°F (200°C, or gas mark 6). In a bowl, toss the zucchini, red pepper, and onion with the olive oil and sea salt. Spread in a roasting pan and roast for 25 to 30 minutes, until the zucchini is tender. Prepare the Black Bean Enchiladas as directed, using the roasted zucchini in conjunction with the beans.

Spinach with Pumpkin Sauce

YIELD: 8 ENCHILADAS

· ·

Pumpkin Sauce
¼ yellow onion
1 cup (245 g) pumpkin purée
¾ cup (180 ml) vegetable broth
2 tablespoons (2 g) chopped cilantro
2 tablespoons (30 ml) freshly squeezed lime juice
½ teaspoon chili powder
½ teaspoon ground cumin
¼ teaspoon salt

1 recipe Black Bean Enchiladas (page 146)
1 cup (40 g) shredded spinach

To make the sauce: Combine the onion, pumpkin purée, and vegetable broth in a small saucepan, then stir in the cilantro, lime juice, chili powder, cumin, and salt. Heat over medium-low heat until warm

Prepare the Black Bean Enchiladas as directed, adding the shredded spinach to the beans and using the pumpkin sauce in place of the tomato sauce.

Spiced Rutabaga

YIELD: 8 ENCHILADAS

· ·

1 recipe Black Bean Enchiladas (page 146)
2 rutabagas, cubed
1 tablespoon (15 ml) olive oil
½ teaspoon cumin
½ teaspoon coriander seeds
1 teaspoon smoked paprika

Preheat the oven to 375°F (190°C, or gas mark 5). In a roasting pan, combine the cubed rutabagas, olive oil, cumin, coriander, and smoked paprika. Bake until the rutabaga is tender, 30 to 35 minutes.

Prepare the Black Bean Enchiladas as directed, using the roasted rutabaga in conjunction with the beans.

6

Desserts

If you take a look at the recipe section on naturallyella.com, you'll notice that I don't post a lot of recipes for sweets. I think that makes my website look healthier than my own eating habits actually are! But as I mentioned earlier, I've always been a major proponent of the old maxim "everything in moderation." It's not that I don't care to bake. In fact, I preferred baking to cooking for quite a long time. I can make a pretty mean cheesecake, and can frost a cake like I've been doing it forever. During the holidays, I'm the official dessert maker, happily whipping up pies and cookies galore. Oh yes, I love my sweets—and this chapter is living proof.

Although chocolate-based desserts are probably my favorite, the seasonal recipes in this chapter make up the majority of desserts that appear on my table. Opting for fruit-based desserts (sometimes) means less sugar—unless the dessert is lemon- or lime-based—and they're also the perfect end to a seasonal meal. You can always eat the fruit plain, or dipped in a little whipped cream, but the recipes here go a few steps further.

For sweeteners, I stick primarily to natural sweeteners such as maple syrup, honey, sorghum, and molasses. Occasionally I use organic cane sugar, mainly for flavor, and confectioners' sugar in the frosting recipes. And as for flour, whole wheat pastry flour is a great substitution for traditional unbleached all-purpose flour. The finely ground pastry flour works as a 1:1 substitute for the all-purpose variety. However, if all-purpose flour is what you have on hand, feel free to use it.

< Cinnamon Pear Custard Tart

Sorbet

My great-aunt lived a few houses down the street from my childhood home. As a kid, I'd traverse the neighbors' backyards until I arrived at her apartment; she'd sometimes watch me while my parents were at work. Our days together were filled with card games, people-watching from her balcony, and food, always food. She was the one who showed me it was okay to love butter, to make a mean batch of potatoes, and to really enjoy the food I was eating. After a big meal, dessert was often a bowl of rainbow sherbet—my favorite.

I still love sherbet, but sorbet is a great homemade replacement for store-bought sherbet. It calls for only a few ingredients, and can easily be whipped up with a bit of puréed fruit or fruit juice. I've experimented with more natural sugars in the base recipe, but I've always found that they overpower the delicate fruit flavors, so I stick to cane sugar here.

The fruit-to-water ratio can be varied in this recipe. I like to bulk it up by using a bit more water, but you can use fruit juice for the same purpose as well. This recipe is also fairly loose when it comes to sugar. For tart flavors, such as lemon and lime, a bit more sweetener goes a long way, but if I'm using fresh berries, I tend to cut back. The best thing to do is taste. Once you've cooked the fruit mixture on the stove top, taste it and add more sweetener if you like.

Fruit Sorbet

YIELD: 6 TO 8 SERVINGS

. . . .

3 cups (720 ml) fruit juice
2½ cups (600 ml) water
½ to 1 cup (100 to 200 g) cane sugar

In a saucepan, whisk together the fruit juice, water, and sugar. Bring to a boil and reduce to a simmer. Let cook for 1 to 2 minutes, until the sugar is fully dissolved. Remove from the heat, transfer to a container, and place in the refrigerator to chill completely.

Freeze the sorbet mixture according to your ice cream maker's directions, or, if not using an ice cream maker, place the mixture in a shallow pan and freeze. Once frozen, break into pieces and purée in a blender or food processor until creamy.

Blackberry Sorbet >

SPRING

Strawberry

YIELD: 6 TO 8 SERVINGS

. . . .

1 recipe Fruit Sorbet (page 152)
4 cups (520 g) quartered strawberries
2½ cups (600 ml) water
3 tablespoons (45 ml) lemon juice
1 teaspoon lemon zest
¼ cup (50 g) sugar

Purée the strawberries, water, and lemon juice together in a blender. Make the Fruit Sorbet as directed, using the strawberry purée in place of the juice mixture and adding the lemon zest and sugar to the saucepan.

 SUMMER

Blackberry

YIELD: 6 TO 8 SERVINGS

. . . .

1 recipe Fruit Sorbet (page 152)
4 cups (560 g) blackberries
2 tablespoons (30 ml) lemon juice

Rinse the blackberries, then combine in a blender with the water and lemon juice. Purée until smooth, then press the mixture through a sieve to grab the seeds. Make the Fruit Sorbet as directed, using the blackberry purée in place of the juice mixture.

 FALL

Pear

YIELD: 6 TO 8 SERVINGS

. . . .

1 recipe Fruit Sorbet (page 152)
2 pounds (908 g) pears, quartered and cored
2½ cups (600 ml) water
½ cup (100 g) sugar

Purée the pears with the water in a blender. Make the Fruit Sorbet as directed, using the pear purée in place of the juice mixture and adding the sugar to the saucepan.

 WINTER

Three-Citrus

YIELD: 6 TO 8 SERVINGS

. . . .

1 recipe Fruit Sorbet (page 152)
1½ cups (360 ml) orange juice
1½ cups (360 ml) tangerine juice
½ cup (120 ml) lemon juice
2¼ cups (540 ml) water
½ to 1 cup (100 to 200 g) cane sugar
Zest from 1 orange

Make the Fruit Sorbet as directed, using the orange juice, tangerine juice, lemon juice, and water as the juice mixture and adding the sugar and zest to the saucepan.

Fresh Fruit Crisp

Early on in the cookbook-writing process, I learned not to ask my mother for help if I needed a couple of extra hands for recipe testing. She'd test a recipe, sure, but then—to my horror—she'd casually mention that she changed one ingredient, and didn't really bother measuring the correct amount of another. I couldn't fault her, though, because when I'm not developing recipes for clients or for my site, that's exactly how I cook. I'm free-handed with everything: a "hefty pinch" of salt, a "drizzle" of olive oil, and "roughly a cup" of chopped vegetables are measurements that pop up frequently in my home cooking. Of course, baking is a different story: measurements usually need to be more precise.

Except for fruit crisps, that is. This crisp recipe was born from my free-handed dessert-making style. I had a bit of fresh fruit, and wanted a warm dessert to serve with vanilla ice cream. It worked—the filling isn't overly sweet, and the topping stays nice and crisp once it's out of the oven. (I prefer using oat flour in my crisp topping, because it adds another dimension of flavor to the overall dessert.)

The base recipe allows for a bit of give-and-take in the quantities of sweetener and flour. If I'm using produce that's on the tart side, such as rhubarb, I'll up the amount of sweetener, or I might balance that tartness by adding a sweeter variety of fruit. For juicy fruits, such as berries, I'll add an extra tablespoon (8 g) of flour to help them thicken. And if your crisp is a little skimpy on flour, don't worry. It'll just have extra juice, which is perfect if you're serving it alongside a scoop of ice cream.

Fruit and Oat Crisp

YIELD: 3 TO 4 SERVINGS

• •

Filling
2½ to 3 cups (375 to 450 g) cut-up fresh fruit
2 tablespoons (30 ml) maple syrup
1 tablespoon (8 g) whole wheat pastry
    or oat flour
1 teaspoon vanilla extract

Topping
½ cup (50 g) oat flour
½ cup (50 g) rolled oats
2 tablespoons (28 g) unsalted butter
1 tablespoons (15 ml) maple syrup

Preheat the oven to 375°F (190°C, or gas mark 5).

To make the filling: Combine the fruit, maple syrup, flour, and vanilla extract in a 2-quart (1.8 L) baking dish. Toss until the fruit is coated.

To make the topping: In a food processor, combine the oat flour and rolled oats. Pulse in the butter and maple syrup until clumps form. Sprinkle the oat clumps over the fruit evenly.

Bake for 25 to 28 minutes, until the topping is golden and the fruit is bubbling. Let cool for 5 minutes before serving.

SPRING

Rhubarb

YIELD: 3 TO 4 SERVINGS

. . . .

1 recipe Fruit and Oat Crisp (page 155)
3 cups (330 g) diced rhubarb
½ cup (120 ml) maple syrup
¼ cup (30 g) all-purpose flour or oat flour
1 teaspoon ground cinnamon

Prepare the Fruit and Oat Crisp as directed, using the rhubarb as the fruit, increasing the maple syrup to ½ cup (120 ml) and the flour to ¼ cup (30 g), and adding in the cinnamon.

 SUMMER

Peach-Cardamom

YIELD: 3 TO 4 SERVINGS

. . . .

1 recipe Fruit and Oat Crisp (page 155)
2½ cups (338 g) peeled and sliced peaches (2 large peaches)
2 tablespoons (30 ml) sorghum
¼ teaspoon cardamom

Prepare the Fruit and Oat Crisp as directed, using the sliced peaches as the fruit, the sorghum in place of the maple syrup, and adding in the cardamom.

 FALL

Plum

YIELD: 3 TO 4 SERVINGS

. . . .

1 recipe Fruit and Oat Crisp (page 155)
2½ cups (338 g) sliced plums (3 plums)
½ teaspoon ground cinnamon

Prepare the Fruit and Oat Crisp as directed, using the sliced plums as the fruit and adding in the cinnamon.

 WINTER

Pumpkin-Apple

YIELD: 3 TO 4 SERVINGS

. . . .

1 recipe Fruit and Oat Crisp (page 155)
2 cups (280 g) cubed pumpkin
½ cup (70 g) peeled and ¼-inch (6 mm) cubed apples
¼ cup (60 ml) maple syrup
1 teaspoon cinnamon
½ teaspoon vanilla extract

Prepare the Fruit and Oat Crisp as directed, using the cubed pumpkin and apples as the fruit, increasing the amount of maple syrup to ¼ cup (60 ml), and adding in the cinnamon and vanilla extract.

< *Rhubarb Oat Crisp*

Cupcakes

When it comes to cupcakes, I employ very strict standards: the cake must be moist but fluffy; the flavor should include a touch of vanilla; and the frosting should be the supporting act, not the star of the show. While there are already plenty of recipes that meet those standards, I wanted to achieve that same consistency with a cupcake base that doesn't involve refined sugar. That's why I use maple syrup here. It adds a hint of flavor without sacrificing the all-important fluffy texture.

I limit the amount of frosting to a mere smear on top of each. If you'd rather pipe on the buttercream frosting—multiply the buttercream frosting recipe by one and a half. If you prefer a lighter frosting, try using the whipped cream version—just be sure to keep the cupcakes refrigerated until serving.

Vanilla Cupcakes

YIELD: 12 CUPCAKES

Cupcakes
2½ cups (300 g) whole-wheat pastry flour
   or unbleached all-purpose flour
2 teaspoons baking powder
½ teaspoon baking soda
½ teaspoon sea salt
2 large eggs
¾ cup (180 ml) maple syrup or brown rice syrup
½ cup (112 g) unsalted butter, melted and cooled
½ cup (120 ml) milk
1 teaspoon vanilla extract

Buttercream Frosting
½ cup (112 g) unsalted butter, softened
2 cups (240 g) confectioners' sugar
1 teaspoon vanilla extract
3 tablespoons (45 ml) heavy cream, divided

Whipped Cream Frosting
1 cup (240 ml) heavy cream
2 tablespoons (30 ml) maple syrup

To make the cupcakes: Preheat the oven to 350˚F (180˚C, or gas mark 4). Line a 12-cup muffin tin with paper liners.

In a large bowl, stir together the flour, baking powder, baking soda, and sea salt. In a separate bowl, whisk together the eggs, maple syrup, melted butter, milk, and vanilla extract. Pour the wet ingredients into the dry and stir until just combined and the lumps are mostly gone.

Using an ice-cream scoop, divide the batter among 12 muffin cups, allowing for about 1 scoop (2¼ ounces [65 g]) of batter for each muffin. Bake the cupcakes for 18 to 22 minutes, until they spring back when pressed and a knife comes out clean when inserted. Remove from the oven, transfer to a wire rack, and let cool completely.

To make the buttercream frosting: In a bowl, beat together the butter, confectioners' sugar, vanilla extract, and 2 tablespoons (30 ml) of the heavy cream until well combined, adding the remaining cream if needed. The frosting should be easily spreadable.

To make the whipped cream frosting: Using a hand mixer or stand mixer, beat the heavy cream until stiff peaks form. Stir in the maple syrup.

Spread the chosen frosting on the cooled cupcakes and serve. Store the cupcakes in an airtight container at room temperature for 2 to 3 days.

SPRING

Strawberry-Filled Cupcakes

YIELD: 12 CUPCAKES

. . . .

Filling

1½ cups (210 g) quartered strawberries
2 tablespoons (30 ml) maple syrup
2 tablespoons (16 g) cornstarch
1 tablespoon (15 ml) water
1 recipe Vanilla Cupcakes (page 158)

To make the filling: Add the strawberries and maple syrup to a saucepan, and cook until the juices release, 7 to 10 minutes. Whisk together the cornstarch and water in a small bowl and pour into the strawberry mixture. Continue to cook, stirring often, until the mixture has thickened, 3 to 4 minutes.

Bake the Vanilla Cupcakes as directed. When the cupcakes have cooled, scoop out part of the top of each cupcake with a paring knife and place a spoonful of strawberry filling inside. Spread the desired frosting on top.

 SUMMER

Lemon Cupcakes with Blueberry Frosting

YIELD: 12 CUPCAKES

. . . .

1 recipe Vanilla Cupcakes (page 158)
½ teaspoon lemon extract
2 teaspoons lemon zest

Frosting

1 recipe Buttercream Frosting (page 158)
1 cup (120 g) blueberries
1 tablespoon (15 ml) lemon juice

Make the Vanilla Cupcakes as directed, adding the lemon extract and zest into the batter with the wet ingredients.

To make the frosting: Pick out 12 perfect blueberries and set aside. Mash the remaining blueberries in a skillet with the lemon juice. Heat over medium heat until the blueberries have released their juices and are soft, 6 to 8 minutes. Press the blueberries through a sieve or cheesecloth, reserving the liquid. Measure out 3 tablespoons (45 ml). Make the Buttercream Frosting as directed, using the blueberry juice in place of the heavy cream. Frost the cupcakes, and top each one with a blueberry.

FALL

Pear Cupcakes with Buttercream Frosting

YIELD: 12 CUPCAKES

. . . .

1 recipe Vanilla Cupcakes (page 158)
1 firm pear, peeled and cored
1 teaspoon ground cinnamon
¼ teaspoon ground nutmeg
1 recipe Buttercream Frosting (page 158)

Shred the pear using a medium box grater. Place the grated pear in a sieve, and press out as much liquid as possible into a bowl. Reserve the liquid. Make the Vanilla Cupcakes as directed, add the squeezed pears to the dry ingredients along with the cinnamon and nutmeg and replacing up to ¼ cup (60 ml) of the milk with the pear juice.

Bake as directed. Check the cupcakes after 18 minutes but, because of the fruit, the cupcakes may take closer to 22 to 24 minutes. Let cool, then frost with the Buttercream Frosting and sprinkle with cinnamon to finish.

 WINTER

Orange Cream Cupcakes

YIELD: 12 CUPCAKES

. . . .

Orange Curd
¼ cup (60 ml) brown rice syrup
2 tablespoons (40 g) honey
2 large eggs
1 egg yolk
¼ cup (30 ml) orange juice, divided
1 teaspoon each cornstarch and orange zest
2 tablespoons (26 g) unsalted butter, softened

1 recipe Vanilla Cupcakes (page 158)
1 recipe Whipped Cream Frosting (page 158)

To make the orange curd: In a bowl, whisk together the brown rice syrup, honey, eggs, and egg yolk. In a separate bowl, whisk together 2 tablespoons (30 ml) of the orange juice and the cornstarch until dissolved. Whisk in the remaining 2 tablespoons (30 ml) juice and the zest. Pour into the egg mixture and whisk again until well combined.

Place the mixture in the top of a double boiler and heat over medium-low heat, whisking constantly, until thickened, 5 to 6 minutes. Remove from the heat and add the butter, whisking until melted and well incorporated. Let cool and thicken.

Make the Vanilla Cupcakes as directed. When the cupcakes have cooled, scoop out part of the top of the cupcake with a paring knife and place a spoonful of orange curd inside. Frost with the Whipped Cream Frosting.

Fruit Compote

By now, you've probably realized that my husband and I have a bit of an ice cream addiction—as evidenced by the number of times I suggest serving ice cream alongside other desserts! We always, and I mean *always*, have ice cream in the freezer, and it's usually vanilla: we don't always agree on flavors, so it's a safe middle ground.

Then we'll each jazz up our dishes of vanilla. My husband will usually grab the jar of peanut butter, while I go for fresh fruit or chocolate. If I'm in the mood for the former, I'll whip up one of these fresh fruit compotes. They come together easily, and, for the most part, don't take that long to cook.

Now, I use the word "compote" loosely here. Basically, it means "some kind of cooked fruit tossed with a bit of sugar." If you don't want your compote to be overly sweet, start with a reduced amount of sugar, taste, then add more as desired. Also, feel free to play with spices here. Cinnamon and cardamom are two of my favorite ways to add flavor to the fruity sweetness. And if I end up with leftover compote, I like to swirl it into a bowl of plain yogurt or add it to one of the crepes beginning on page 168.

Ginger Pear Compote

Seasonal Fruit Compote

YIELD: 1 TO 1½ CUPS (240 TO 320 G)

• •

2 cups (300 g) diced fruit
2 tablespoons (30 ml) maple syrup
2 tablespoons (24 g) muscovado sugar
¼ teaspoon vanilla extract

Combine all the ingredients in a small pot and simmer over low heat until the fruit is soft and is starting to break down, 6 to 8 minutes. Let cool slightly before serving.

SPRING

Oven-Roasted Rhubarb and Clove

YIELD: ½ CUP (120 G)

• •

1 recipe Seasonal Fruit Compote (page 161)
2 cups (220 g) diced rhubarb
¼ teaspoon ground cloves

Preheat the oven to 375°F (190°C, or gas mark 5). Combine all the ingredients for the Seasonal Fruit Compote in a roasting pan, using the rhubarb as the fruit and adding in the cloves. Cover with foil and roast for 30 to 35 minutes, until the rhubarb breaks down and reaches the texture of a thick sauce. Let cool slightly before serving.

 SUMMER

Raspberry

YIELD: 1 CUP (240 G)

• •

1 recipe Seasonal Fruit Compote (page 161)
2 cups (240 g) raspberries
1 tablespoon (15 ml) bourbon
¼ teaspoon ground cardamom

Prepare the Seasonal Fruit Compote as directed, using the raspberries as the fruit and adding in the bourbon and cardamom. Cook for 10 to 12 minutes.

 FALL

Apple Cinnamon

YIELD: 1 CUP (240 G)

• •

1 recipe Seasonal Fruit Compote (page 161)
2 cups (240 g) peeled, cubed apples
1 teaspoon cinnamon
¼ cup (60 ml) maple syrup

Preheat the oven to 400°F (200°C, or gas mark 6). Combine all the ingredients for the Seasonal Fruit Compote in a roasting pan, using the cubed apples as the fruit, adding in the cinnamon, and using ¼ cup (60 ml) maple syrup instead of the 2 tablespoons (30 ml). Roast for 20 to 25 minutes, until the apples are tender, then mash with a fork or purée in a food processor. Let cool slightly before serving.

 WINTER

Ginger Pear

YIELD: 1 CUP (240 G)

• •

2 cups (240 g) peeled and ¼-inch (6 mm) cubed pears
3 tablespoons (60 g) honey
1 tablespoon (15 ml) lemon juice
2 teaspoons minced fresh ginger

Combine the ingredients in a skillet or saucepan. Cook over low heat until the pears are soft, 10 to 12 minutes. Let cool slightly before serving.

< Oven-Roasted Rhubarb and Clove Compote

Baked Cream Tart

I grew up in a family of pie lovers. At every holiday, at every special occasion, there were pies. Single-crust, double-crust, lattice-crust, you name, we had it. And yet, when I started teaching myself more about baking, I gravitated toward tarts. The crust's beautiful edge has a certain elegance, as does its simple (not overly stuffed) filling. As I kept baking, I delved deeper into the world of tarts, including chocolate and curd varieties, and this cream tart.

Making puddings and custard bases can be a bit tricky when it comes to controlling the heat. You have to be careful not to scorch the bottom. This tart takes the work out of that because the custard is baked right in the crust. The hardest part of this tart is making the crust, and if you've mastered that, you'll see that it comes together in no time.

As for fillings, I nearly always bake the fruit into the filling, unless I'm using fresh fruit that deserves to remain raw, like fresh berries. Also, this tart is one of the richer desserts in this book, and could easily be cut into 12 small-but-satisfying pieces.

Basic Custard Tart

YIELD: 8 TO 10 SERVINGS

. . . .

Crust
1¼ cups (150 g) unbleached all-purpose flour
  or whole-wheat pastry flour
¼ teaspoon sea salt
6 tablespoons (84 g) cold unsalted butter
1 ounce (28 g) cream cheese
2 tablespoons (30 ml) maple syrup
2 tablespoons (30 ml) cold water

Cream Filling
½ cup (60 g) unbleached all-purpose flour
  or whole-wheat pastry flour
½ cup (120 ml) maple syrup
6 large eggs
¼ cup (60 ml) heavy cream
1 teaspoon vanilla extract
2 tablespoons (28 g) unsalted butter,
  melted and cooled

2 cups (300 g) fruit or berries

Preheat the oven to 375°F (190°C, or gas mark 5).

To make the crust: In a food processor or bowl, combine the flour and salt. Cut or pulse in the butter and cream cheese until the dough is in pea-sized pieces. Stir or pulse in the maple syrup and cold water until the dough comes together.

Transfer the dough to a floured work surface and roll into a circle large enough to cover an 11-inch (28 cm) tart pan. Transfer and press the dough into the tart pan. Pierce the bottom with a fork and parbake the crust for 10 minutes, until it is lightly golden.

To make the cream filling: Combine the filling ingredients in a blender and process until smooth. Sprinkle the fruit over the crust, pour the cream filling over, and return the tart to the oven. Bake for 20 to 25 minutes, until the custard is set and lightly browned. Remove from the oven and let cool.

Strawberry Lime Custard Tart >

SPRING

Strawberry Lime

YIELD: 8 TO 10 SERVINGS

. . . .

1 recipe Basic Custard Tart (page 164)

Lime Curd
¾ cup (180 ml) maple syrup
4 large eggs
2 egg yolks
½ cup (120 ml) lime juice, divided
2 teaspoons cornstarch
1 teaspoon lime zest
4 tablespoons (56 g) unsalted butter, softened
¾ pound (340 g) fresh strawberries

Prepare the Basic Custard Tart Crust as directed.

To make the curd: Whisk together the maple syrup, eggs, and yolks. In a separate bowl, whisk 2 tablespoons (30 ml) of the lime juice with the cornstarch until dissolved. Whisk in the remaining lime juice and zest. Pour into the egg mixture and whisk until well combined.

Place the mixture in the top of a double boiler and heat over medium-low heat, whisking constantly, until thickened, 5 to 6 minutes. Remove from the heat and add the butter, whisking until melted and well incorporated. Pour the custard into the baked tart crust and let cool. Once cool, slice the strawberries and layer over the curd. Chill in the refrigerator until ready to serve.

 SUMMER

Raspberry

YIELD: 8 TO 10 SERVINGS

. . . .

1 recipe Basic Custard Tart (page 164)
¾ pound (340 g) mixed golden, red, and black raspberries

Prepare the Basic Custard Tart as directed, baking the custard without the fruit. Let cool. Top with the raspberries.

 FALL

Cinnamon Pear

YIELD: 8 TO 10 SERVINGS

. . . .

1 recipe Basic Custard Tart (page 164)
1 teaspoon ground cinnamon
1 large, firm pear

Prepare the Basic Custard Tart as directed, adding the cinnamon to the filling. Cut the pear into ¼-inch (6 mm) slices and layer on the parbaked crust. Pour the custard filling over the pears and bake as directed.

 WINTER

Vanilla Bean and Pomegranate

YIELD: 8 TO 10 SERVINGS

. . . .

1 recipe Basic Custard Tart (page 164)
2 vanilla beans
1 cup (160 g) pomegranate arils

Prepare the Basic Custard Tart as directed, replacing the vanilla extract with seeds scraped from the vanilla beans. Spread the pomegranate arils over the parbaked crust. Pour the custard filling over the arils and bake as directed.

Cinnamon Pear Custard Tart >

Crepes

There's a restaurant with amazing crepes in the small town where my husband and I used to live. Our date nights usually went something like this: we'd go out to dinner, then see a show or walk around downtown—and then, inevitably, we'd end up at the crepe place before heading home. The restaurant has a lovely outdoor patio where we'd linger over a late-night coffee, sharing an incredible dessert crepe filled with ice cream and smothered with fruit or a sweet sauce, or both.

Then we moved to California, and I decided to recreate those wonderful crepes at home. And I found that they look harder to make than they actually are. What's the key to great crepes? Good batter consistency and a nonstick skillet. It may take a few tries to get them right, but once you get the hang of them, crepes become quick and easy to make, and are a great recipe to reach for in a pinch. I've also used this crepe base for savory fillings, often to replace the bread in the grilled cheese sandwiches on page 51.

The thing I love most about crepes is that it's easy to make flour substitutions and still end up with great results. I often use rye flour instead of the whole wheat pastry flour, or sometimes I make gluten-free crepes by using oat flour. And the combinations of crepes and fillings are limitless—you can stuff them with just about anything. Even better, crepes freeze well for quick use. Just separate the crepes with parchment paper, and place them in the freezer in an airtight container for up to a month.

Whole-Grain Crepes

YIELD: 8 CREPES

½ cup (60 g) whole wheat pastry flour
¼ teaspoon salt
2 large eggs
1 tablespoon (15 ml) maple syrup
½ cup (120 ml) milk
1 tablespoon (14 g) unsalted butter, melted

In a medium bowl, whisk together the flour, salt, eggs, maple syrup, milk, and butter until smooth. Heat an 8-inch (20 cm) nonstick skillet over medium-low heat and lightly brush with melted butter. Pour a scant ¼ cup (60 ml) of batter into the skillet. Working quickly, tilt the skillet in a circle so that the batter covers the entire bottom, and cook for 1 minute. Flip and cook for another 30 to 60 seconds. The crepe should be lightly browned on each side. Layer the finished crepes, slightly overlapping, on a plate.

 Adjust the heat setting as you go. You may need to reduce it slightly as the pan gets hot.

Lemon Curd Crepes >

SPRING

Lemon Curd

YIELD: 1 CUP (240 G) CURD (ENOUGH FILLING FOR 8 CREPES)

. . . .

1 recipe Whole-Grain Crepes (page 168)
¼ cup (30 g) rye flour

Lemon Curd
¼ cup (60 ml) brown rice syrup
2 tablespoons (40 g) honey
2 large eggs
1 egg yolk
¼ cup (60 ml) lemon juice, divided
1 teaspoon cornstarch
1 teaspoon lemon zest
2 tablespoons (28 g) unsalted butter, softened
¼ to ½ cup (60 to 120 g) mascarpone cheese

Prepare the Whole-Grain Crepes as directed, using ¼ cup (30 g) rye flour in place of ¼ cup (30 g) whole wheat flour.

To make the curd: In a bowl, whisk together the brown rice syrup, honey, eggs, and egg yolk. In a separate bowl, whisk together 2 tablespoons (30 ml) of the lemon juice with the cornstarch until dissolved. Whisk in the remaining 2 table-spoons (30 ml) lemon juice and the zest. Pour into the egg mixture and whisk again until well combined.

Place the mixture in the top of a double boiler and heat over medium-low heat, whisking constantly, until thickened, 5 to 6 minutes. Remove from the heat and add the butter, whisking until melted and well incorporated.

To assemble crepes, smear 1 to 2 tablespoons (15 to 30 g) mascarpone cheese and 2 to 3 tablespoons (30 to 45 g) curd on each as filling.

 This recipe produces a rather thick curd. If you prefer a slightly thinner curd, leave out the cornstarch.

 SUMMER

Fresh Melon with Honey Mint and Simple Syrup

YIELD: 8 CREPES

. . . .

1 just-ripe cantaloupe (about 2 pounds, or 908 g)

Simple Syrup
½ cup (160 g) honey
½ cup (120 ml) water
¼ cup (24 g) minced fresh mint leaves, plus more for garnish

1 recipe Whole-Grain Crepes (page 168)

Peel and seed the cantaloupe. Cut into slices as thin as possible.

To make the simple syrup: In a small pot or skillet, combine the simple syrup ingredients over low heat, simmering until well combined. Turn off the heat and let sit while making the crepes. Strain out the mint.

Prepare the Whole-Grain Crepes as directed, and assemble by filling each with the sliced melon and a drizzle of the mint simple syrup. Garnish with fresh finely chopped mint.

Yogurt, Apples, and Honey

YIELD: 8 CREPES

. . . .

1 recipe Whole-Grain Crepes (page 168)
½ cup plus 1½ tablespoons (60 g) oat flour
2 large baking apples, cored and thinly sliced
3 tablespoons (60 g) honey, divided
2 tablespoons (30 ml) lemon juice
1 teaspoon minced fresh ginger
1 cup (240 g) plain Greek-style yogurt

Prepare the Whole-Grain Crepes as directed, using the oat flour in place of the wheat flour.

In a skillet or saucepan, combine the apples with 2 tablespoons (40 g) of the honey, lemon juice, and ginger. Cover and let cook until tender, 5 to 6 minutes. In a small bowl, stir together the Greek yogurt and remaining 1 tablespoon (20 g) of honey.

To assemble the crepes, smear 2 tablespoons (30 g) each of the filling and the Greek yogurt mixture on each crepe.

 I like my apples skin-on, but if you prefer them skinless, just peel before thinly slicing.

Stewed Oranges, Cardamom, and Crème Fraîche

YIELD: 8 CREPES

. . . .

1 recipe Whole-Grain Crepes (page 168)
2 navel or Valencia oranges
2 tablespoons (30 ml) sorghum syrup
¼ teaspoon cardamom
½ to 1 cup (120 to 240 g) crème fraîche

Prepare the Whole-Grain Crepes as directed.

Peel the orange and divide into sections, removing any white pith. Add the oranges to a small saucepan with the sorghum and cardamom. Cook over medium heat until tender and the juice has partially released, 4 to 5 minutes, smashing them with back of the spoon to help the process along.

Assemble the crepes by smearing 1 to 2 tablespoons (15 to 30 g) of crème fraîche on each crepe and topping with a spoonful of the cooked orange mixture.

Fresh Fruit Galette

I alternate the flours I use when making galettes. I love the earthiness that whole wheat flour lends to the dessert, especially when paired with the mixed berries of summer and the fresh pumpkin of fall. The key to this crust is to make sure the butter is in pieces that are small enough not to get messy while baking, but that can still create that flaky pie crust texture. For this very reason, I love using the food processor instead of my hands because the less handling the dough gets, the better.

The main recipe has specific instructions for the crust, but it's a bit harder to specify exact amounts for the fillings. Some fillings that aren't extremely juicy, such as rhubarb, will require a different flour-to-sweetener ratio than juicy fruits, such as cranberry, will. Use your best judgment when you're making the variations listed here. Just be sure to use a rimmed baking sheet and parchment paper for easy cleanup in case the filling doesn't set.

Dessert Galette

YIELD: 6 SERVINGS

Crust

1 cup (120 g) unbleached all-purpose flour
  or whole wheat pastry flour
¼ teaspoon sea salt
¼ cup (56 g) cold unsalted butter
1 ounce (28 g) cream cheese
1 tablespoon (15 ml) maple syrup
2 tablespoons (30 ml) cold water

Filling

2½ to 3 cups (375 to 450 g) cubed fruit
3 tablespoons (45 ml) maple syrup
3 tablespoons (24 g) unbleached all-purpose
  flour or whole wheat pastry flour

Egg Wash

2 tablespoons (30 ml) heavy cream
1 large egg

Preheat the oven to 375˚F (190˚C, or gas mark 5). Line a baking sheet with parchment paper.

To make the crust: In a food processor or large bowl, combine the flour and salt. Cut in the butter and cream cheese, pulsing in a food processor or using your fingers until the dough is in pea-sized pieces. Add the maple syrup and water, pulsing or stirring until the dough comes together. Turn out onto a floured work surface and roll the dough into a 10-inch (25 cm) circle. Transfer to the prepared baking sheet.

To make the filling: In a bowl, combine the filling ingredients. Spread the filling on the crust, leaving roughly a 1½-inch (3.8 cm) border all the way around. Fold the edges of the crust over the outer edges of the fruit, pleating as needed to make an even circle.

To make the egg wash: Whisk together the cream and egg, then brush the crust with the egg wash.

Transfer to the oven and bake for 35 to 40 minutes, until the crust is golden and the filling is set and bubbling. Remove from the oven and let cool before serving. Store leftovers in an airtight container in the refrigerator for 3 to 4 days.

Mini-Galettes with Spiced Rhubarb and Walnut >

SPRING

Mini-Galettes with Spiced Rhubarb and Walnut

YIELD: 8 SERVINGS

- -

1 recipe Dessert Galette Crust (page 172)

Filling
2 cups (220 g) diced rhubarb
½ cup (50 g) chopped walnuts
¼ cup (60 ml) maple syrup
2 tablespoons (15 g) flour
½ teaspoon vanilla extract
½ teaspoon cinnamon
¼ teaspoon ground cloves
¼ teaspoon ground ginger

1 recipe Dessert Galette Egg Wash (page 172)

Prepare the Dessert Galette Crust as directed, but instead of transferring it whole to the baking tray, use a 3-inch (7.5 cm) cookie cutter or equivalent to cut out 8 circles. Transfer the smaller circles to the baking tray.

To make the filling: In a bowl, toss together the filling ingredients and combine until the rhubarb is coated. Divide the filling among the crust circles, leaving a ½ inch (1.3 cm) border. Fold the edges of the crust over the outer edges of the fruit, pleating as needed to make an even circle. Brush with the egg wash. Adjust the baking time to 30 to 35 minutes.

 To make this variation as one larger galette, make as directed for the Dessert Galette.

 SUMMER

Mixed Berry

YIELD: 6 SERVINGS

- -

1 recipe Dessert Galette Crust (page 172)
3 cups (375 g) mixed summer berries
1 teaspoon lemon zest
1 recipe Dessert Galette Egg Wash (page 172)

Prepare the Dessert Galette as directed, using the mixed berries and lemon zest as the filling. Brush with the egg wash before baking.

 Try using just-ripe berries: they'll hold their shape better than older, overly ripe ones.

FALL

Pumpkin

YIELD: 6 SERVINGS

. . . .

1 recipe Dessert Galette Crust (page 172)

Filling

1 cup (245 g) pumpkin purée
6 ounces (168 g) cream cheese, at room temperature
¼ cup (60 ml) maple syrup
1 large egg
1 teaspoon cinnamon
¼ teaspoon ground ginger
¼ teaspoon ground cloves
¼ teaspoon ground nutmeg

1 recipe Dessert Galette Egg Wash (page 172)

Prepare the crust as directed and transfer to a 9-inch (23 cm) pie pan.

To make the filling: In a food processor or large bowl, beat together the ingredients for the filling until smooth and well combined. Continue with Dessert Galette recipe, using pumpkin mixture as the filling and brushing with the egg wash.

 WINTER

Cranberry

YIELD: 6 SERVINGS

. . . .

1 recipe Dessert Galette Crust (page 172)

Filling

2½ cups (265 g) cranberries (if using frozen, thaw)
½ cup (86 g) sucanat
¼ cup plus 2 tablespoons (45 g) flour
¼ cup (60 ml) maple syrup
1 teaspoon ground cinnamon

1 recipe Dessert Galette Egg Wash (page 172)

Prepare the Dessert Galette Crust as directed.

To make the filling: In a saucepan, heat the cranberries over medium-low heat until they begin to release their juices, 4 to 5 minutes. As the cranberries warm, mash them gently with the back of a spoon. Stir in the remaining filling ingredients and cook until the mixture has thickened, 3 to 4 minutes.

Continue with Dessert Galette recipe, using the cranberry mixture as the filling. Brush with the egg wash before baking.

Pudding

I'm slightly ashamed to admit there was a time in my life when I swore that pudding was nearly impossible to make at home. I relied far too heavily on those prepackaged individual pudding cups. I packed them in my lunch and ate them as snacks. Chocolate-vanilla swirl was my favorite—although, let's be honest, I wasn't terribly picky. But the first time I tried homemade pudding, my proverbial socks were knocked off—and with a single bite, I swore to never eat the packaged stuff again.

Made with whole milk and chocolate, that first homemade pudding was nothing if not rich and satisfying, and it started my entire pudding experience off on a very positive note. From there, I began experimenting at home with various flavors and types of unrefined sugars. The base recipe here calls for honey, but I use maple syrup just as often, especially when my puddings feature fall fruits. I also like to make sure my pudding isn't overly sweet. That way, the fruit really gets to shine.

This vanilla pudding recipe is a great base to expand upon, but I highly recommend using whole milk and good-quality vanilla extract. The whole milk makes the pudding amazingly creamy, while the vanilla supplies the flavor. Beyond the variations I suggest here, this pudding makes a great showcase for fresh summer berries—black raspberries are my favorite.

Vanilla Bean Pudding

YIELD: 4 TO 5 SERVINGS

· ·

4 large egg yolks
¼ cup (80 g) honey
2 tablespoons (16 g) cornstarch
¼ teaspoon salt
1 vanilla bean
2 cups (480 ml) whole milk
2 tablespoons (28 g) unsalted butter

In a large bowl, whisk together the egg yolks, honey, cornstarch, and salt. Scrape out the vanilla bean seeds into a saucepan, then add the pod to the pan along with the milk. Heat over medium-low heat until the milk is hot but not boiling. Remove the vanilla bean pod.

Temper the eggs by whisking ¼ cup (60 ml) of the hot milk into the mixture, then, in a slow, steady stream, continue to whisk the milk into the egg mixture. Transfer the milk-egg mixture back to the saucepan and turn the heat down to low. Cook, stirring and scraping the bottom of the saucepan often with a spatula, until the pudding has thickened and coats the back of a wooden spoon, 6 to 8 minutes. Remove from the heat and stir in the butter until melted and combined. Serve immediately, or store in an airtight container and chill in the refrigerator.

💬 *Pay close attention when you're cooking the pudding mixture or else it may scorch on the bottom of the saucepan.*

Roasted Cherry Vanilla Bean Pudding >

SPRING

Strawberry

YIELD: 4 TO 5 SERVINGS

. . . .

1 recipe Vanilla Bean Pudding (page 176)
2 cups (240 g) ripe strawberries, hulled and quartered
¼ cup (60 ml) maple syrup

Mash the strawberries and set aside. Prepare the Vanilla Bean Pudding as directed, using the maple syrup in place of the honey. Stir in the mashed strawberries with the butter at the end, and serve warm or chilled.

 If the strawberries aren't very soft, try roasting them as you would the cherries in the summer variation below.

 SUMMER

Roasted Cherry

YIELD: 4 TO 5 SERVINGS

. . . .

1 recipe Vanilla Bean Pudding (page 176)
¾ pound (340 g) cherries, pitted and quartered
3 tablespoons (45 ml) maple syrup
¼ teaspoon vanilla extract

Prepare the Vanilla Bean Pudding as directed.

Preheat the oven to 425°F (220°C, or gas mark 7). In a bowl, toss the cherries with the maple syrup and vanilla extract. Spread in a roasting pan and bake until tender, 15 to 18 minutes. Remove from the oven and stir into the pudding, or keep separate and top the pudding before serving.

 FALL

Pomegranate

YIELD: 4 TO 5 SERVINGS

. . . .

1 recipe Vanilla Bean Pudding (page 176)
¾ cup (180 ml) pomegranate juice
1 tablespoon (20 g) honey
2 tablespoons (16 g) cornstarch
1 tablespoon (15 ml) warm water
¼ cup (40 g) pomegranate arils

Prepare the Vanilla Bean Pudding as directed. In a small saucepan, combine the pomegranate juice and honey. Combine the cornstarch and water in a small bowl, stirring to dissolve the cornstarch. Pour the cornstarch mixture into the pomegranate mixture and heat over low heat, stirring often, until the mixture has thickened and has lost the cloudiness from the cornstarch, 4 to 5 minutes. Swirl the pomegranate mixture and arils into the pudding. Serve while still warm or chill.

 WINTER

Sweet Potato

YIELD: 4 TO 5 SERVINGS

. . . .

1 cup (150 g) ½-inch (1.3 cm) peeled and cubed
    sweet potatoes
1 tablespoon (15 ml) heavy cream
1 teaspoon cinnamon
¼ teaspoon nutmeg
⅛ teaspoon mace
1 recipe Vanilla Bean Pudding (page 176)
¼ cup (60 ml) maple syrup

Bring a saucepan of water to a boil, add the sweet potatoes, and cook until soft, 6 to 8 minutes. Drain, transfer to a food processor along with the heavy cream, cinnamon, nutmeg, and mace, and purée.

Prepare the Vanilla Bean Pudding as directed, using the maple syrup in place of the honey and stirring in the sweet potato mixture at the end.

Cake

It's physically impossible for me to show up empty-handed to a party. Most of the time, I come armed with a bottle of wine, some olives, and a freshly made batch of hummus. Talking about food, I find, is one of the best ways to break the ice when you meet new people—and goodness knows that's no problem for me, because really, I could talk about food all day. And one of the best ways I know to ease your way into new situations is to arrive with a cake in hand. Specifically, *this* cake.

While I love to frost the occasional cake, I don't always have the time. Enter this upside-down cake. It's truly my favorite make-and-go cake. It takes little in the way of preparation, it doesn't need frosting, and the cooked fruit on the top makes for a beautiful presentation. Hands down, it's the best way I know to showcase California's gorgeous citrus fruits. This cake also makes a great road trip or picnic snack, because it packs well and will last for a couple of days in an airtight container at room temperature.

The base recipe allows for unbleached all-purpose flour or whole wheat pastry flour, but I highly recommend using the whole wheat flour because the maple syrup, wheat flour, and fruit topping make a wonderful threesome. As for the fruit, I usually choose not to peel it, but I always make sure I buy organic and rinse the fruit well before using, especially with citrus.

Fruit Upside-Down Cake

YIELD: ONE 8-INCH (20 CM) CAKE, 8 TO 10 SERVINGS

. . . .

Fruit Topping
¼ cup (60 ml) maple syrup
10 to 12 ounces (280 to 336 g) fresh fruit

Cake
1½ cups (180 g) unbleached all-purpose flour
  or whole wheat pastry flour
1 teaspoon baking powder
½ teaspoon baking soda
¼ teaspoon sea salt
2 large eggs
½ cup (112 g) unsalted butter, melted and cooled
½ cup (120 ml) maple syrup
½ cup (120 ml) whole milk

Preheat the oven to 375°F (190°C, or gas mark 5).

To make the fruit topping: In an 8-inch (20 cm) cake pan, add the maple syrup and place in the heated oven until warm, 1 to 2 minutes. Remove from the oven and layer the fresh fruit on the bottom of the pan.

To make the cake: In a bowl, stir together the flour, baking powder, baking soda, and sea salt. In a separate bowl, whisk together the eggs, butter, maple syrup, and whole milk. Pour the wet ingredients into the dry, and stir until well combined and most lumps are gone.

Pour the batter over the fruit and spread evenly using a spatula. Bake for 28 to 32 minutes, until the cake has domed and a knife comes out clean when inserted. Remove from the oven and let cool for 10 minutes. Loosen the edges of the cake with a knife, place a cake plate on top, and in one quick movement, flip onto the cake plate.

Store in an airtight container at room temperature for 2 to 3 days or freeze for extended storage.

SPRING

Honey Orange

YIELD: ONE 8-INCH (20 CM) CAKE, 8 TO 10 SERVINGS

. . . .

1 recipe Fruit Upside-Down Cake (page 179)
½ cup (160 g) honey
½ teaspoon ground cardamom
1 navel, Valencia, or Cara Cara orange

Prepare the Fruit Upside-Down Cake as directed, slicing the orange into ⅛-inch (3 mm) slices and layering on the bottom of the pan over the maple syrup, substituting the honey for the maple syrup in the cake, and adding the cardamom to the dry ingredients.

 The honey will cause this cake to brown more quickly than the other variations, so start checking the cake after about 20 minutes, and cover with foil if the cake is browning too quickly.

 SUMMER

Nectarine

YIELD: ONE 8-INCH (20 CM) CAKE, 8 TO 10 SERVINGS

. . . .

1 recipe Fruit Upside-Down Cake (page 179)
2 small nectarines
¼ cup slivered almonds

Quarter the nectarines and remove the pits. Cut each quarter into ⅛-inch (3 mm) slices. Prepare the Fruit Upside-Down Cake as directed, using the sliced nectarines as the fruit topping. After flipping the cake, top with the almonds.

 If you'd rather use peaches, choose peaches that aren't overly ripe so that they'll still slice well.

FALL

Chai Apple

YIELD: ONE 8-INCH (20 CM) CAKE, 8 TO 10 SERVINGS

. . . .

1 recipe Fruit Upside-Down Cake (page 179)
4 black tea bags
1 whole star anise
1 teaspoon ground cinnamon
½ teaspoon ground ginger
¼ teaspoon ground cloves
¼ teaspoon ground cardamom
¼ teaspoon black pepper
⅛ teaspoon nutmeg
½ large Gala apple, cut into ¼-inch (6 mm) slices

In a saucepan, combine the butter, maple syrup, and milk from the original recipe with the tea bags and spices. Heat until the butter has melted and the milk is hot but not boiling. Remove from the heat and allow to cool until the mixture is lukewarm. Remove the star anise and tea bags, squeezing to remove any extra liquid. Continue with the Fruit Upside-Down Cake as directed, whisking the milk mixture with the eggs and using the apples as the fruit.

 WINTER

Lemon

YIELD: ONE 8-INCH (20 CM) CAKE, 8 TO 10 SERVINGS

. . . .

1 recipe Fruit Upside-Down Cake (page 179)
½ cup (120 ml) sorghum syrup
1 Meyer lemon, thinly sliced

Prepare the Fruit Upside-Down Cake as directed, using the sorghum syrup in place of the maple syrup in the cake and the thinly sliced lemons as the fruit.

 If sorghum syrup is unavailable, use half molasses and half maple syrup instead.

Bread Pudding

There are a few dessert-related gaps in my childhood. During the holidays, I loved going to parties that were filled with cookies, because my favorite, a no-bake cookie, was one my mother never made. Bread pudding also falls into this category, and it wasn't until I was photographing a local café that I even tried it. I finally tasted what I'd been missing. The bread pudding was warm, the custard-like texture was perfect, and the drizzle of heavy cream sent it straight into the realm of the divine. I still dream about that first bite of bread pudding.

My version, though, is a little healthier than the first one I tried. Most of the time, I opt for a whole-grain bread, go easy on the sweetener, and load up on the fruit for extra bulk. Bread pudding is a quick dessert, and I always have all the ingredients on hand. Because my husband isn't a huge bread eater, we often have plenty of stale bread lying around.

Bread pudding is best served straight out of the oven, but can easily be reheated, and I seriously recommend serving it with a drizzle of heavy cream. Also, don't be afraid to experiment with different types of bread. I've made bread pudding with rye bread before, which is surprisingly good, especially when it's garnished with a few fresh berries.

Whole-Grain Bread Pudding

YIELD: 4 SERVINGS

3 cups (180 g) ½-inch (1.3 cm) cubed
   whole-grain bread
3 large eggs
1 cup (240 ml) whole milk
3 tablespoons (45 ml) maple syrup
2 tablespoons (28 g) unsalted butter,
   melted and cooled
½ teaspoon vanilla extract
Heavy cream, for drizzling

Preheat the oven to 350°F (180°C, or gas mark 4). Place the bread cubes in a 1- or 1½-quart (1 or 1.3 L) baking dish. In a bowl, whisk the eggs and then add the milk, maple syrup, melted butter, and vanilla extract. Pour over the bread, pressing the bread down with the back of a spoon to cover with the egg mixture.

Bake the bread pudding for 40 to 45 minutes, until golden and set. Remove from the oven, drizzle with cream, and serve.

 To reheat bread pudding, cover it with foil and place in a 325°F (170°C, or gas mark 3) oven for 12 to 15 minutes until the center is warm.

Apricot Bread Pudding >

SPRING

Apricot

YIELD: 4 SERVINGS

. . . .

1 recipe Whole-Grain Bread Pudding (page 182)
3 tablespoons (45 ml) sorghum syrup
½ teaspoon cardamom
1½ cups (240 g) sliced apricots (3 or 4 apricots)
½ cup (50 g) crushed hazelnuts

Prepare the Bread Pudding as directed, substituting the sorghum syrup for the maple syrup and adding the cardamom to the wet ingredients. Toss the sliced apricots and crushed hazelnuts with the bread cubes before adding the wet ingredients. Bake as directed.

 SUMMER

Blackberry Almond

YIELD: 4 SERVINGS

. . . .

1 recipe Whole-Grain Bread Pudding (page 182)
1½ cups (180 g) blackberries
½ cup (55 g) sliced almonds

Prepare the Bread Pudding as directed, tossing the blackberries and almonds with the bread cubes before adding the wet ingredients. Bake as directed.

 FALL

Apple Bourbon

YIELD: 4 SERVINGS

. . . .

1 recipe Whole-Grain Bread Pudding (page 182)
2 tablespoons (30 ml) bourbon
1 vanilla bean
1 medium-size apple, peeled and cubed
2 tablespoons (22 g) sucanat, for topping before baking

Prepare the Bread Pudding as directed, adding the bourbon and scraping the vanilla bean into the wet ingredients. Toss the apple chunks with the bread cubes before adding the wet ingredients. Sprinkle with the sucanat before baking. Bake as directed.

 If you can't find sucanat, use brown sugar instead.

 WINTER

Spiced Pumpkin

YIELD: 4 SERVINGS

. . . .

1 recipe Whole-Grain Bread Pudding (page 182)
1 cup (245 g) pumpkin purée
2 teaspoons ground cinnamon
¼ teaspoon ground nutmeg
¼ teaspoon ground cloves

Prepare the Bread Pudding as directed, substituting the pumpkin purée for ½ cup (120 ml) of the milk and adding the spices to the wet ingredients.

Blackberry Almond Bread Pudding >

Appendix

Grain Cooking Times

I cook lots of grains as I'd cook pasta: in water with a bit of salt, boiled or simmered until tender, checking occasionally until the grain reaches the right consistency. Also, for extra flavor, I like to toast the grains over medium-low heat in a dry skillet or in a skillet with bit of butter, for 5 to 6 minutes, until the grains have a nice, earthy fragrance.

Wheat Berries/Farro/Kamut/Einkorn/Spelt/Rye/Oat Groats
Place 1 cup (200 g) wheat berries in a stockpot and cover with water, as you would with pasta. Bring to a boil, reduce to a simmer, cover, and let cook until the wheat berries are tender but still a bit chewy, 45 to 55 minutes. After 30 minutes, check the wheat berries regularly. Drain and use as desired. Pearled versions of the grain will cook quicker so start checking them after 25 minutes. Follow these directions for the other grains listed. Weights will vary according to each grain.

Barley
Place 1 cup (185 g) hulled barley in a stockpot and cover with water, as you would with pasta. Bring to a boil, reduce to a simmer, cover, and let cook until the barley is tender but still a bit chewy, 40 to 50 minutes. Drain and use as desired. Pearl barley will cook quicker so start checking it after 20 minutes.

Brown Rice
Place 1 cup (190 g) brown rice in stockpot and cover with water, as you would with pasta. Bring to a boil, reduce to a simmer, cover, and let cook until the rice is tender, 35 to 40 minutes for short grain and 45 to 50 minutes for long grain.

Quinoa
Place 1 cup (175 g) quinoa in a saucepan with 2 cups (470 ml) water. Bring to a boil, reduce to a simmer, cover, and let cook for 10 minutes, or until most of the water has been absorbed. Turn off the heat and allow the quinoa to sit for 10 minutes, then fluff with a fork and serve.

Millet
Place 1 cup (220 g) millet in a saucepan with 2 cups (470 ml) water. Bring to a boil, reduce to a simmer, cover, and let cook for 15 minutes, or until most of the water has been absorbed. Turn off the heat and allow the millet to sit for 10 minutes, then fluff with a fork and serve.

Amaranth
Place 1 cup (185 g) amaranth in a saucepan with 2½ cups (590 ml) water. Bring to a boil, reduce to a simmer, cover, and let cook for 20 minutes, or until most of the water has been absorbed. Turn off the heat and allow the amaranth to sit for 10 minutes before serving.

Polenta
See page 57.

Acknowledgments

To my husband, Mike, for being my chief recipe tester and championing me on during the tough times. To my parents for continuing to inspire me and also for being my biggest cheerleaders. To my grandparents, who might not always understand exactly what it is I do but still get excited about everything. To Erika and Stephanie Cline, Melissa Coleman, April Holland, Kathryne Taylor, Ashley McLaughlin, and Shanna and Tim Mallon for testing out the recipes. And to the team at Fair Winds, including Jill Alexander, Cara Connors, Heather Godin, and my editors, Megan Buckley and Karen Levy, for helping me take a small idea and make it into a wonderful book.

About the Author

Photographer and Web designer Erin Alderson is the voice behind Naturally Ella, a whole foods, vegetarian blog that features accessible, healthy recipes. Erin's work has been featured on The Kitchn, *Food and Wine*, Food52, and *Bon Appétit*. When not creating a mess in the kitchen, Erin can be found in the mountains hiking or snowboarding. She currently resides in Sacramento, California, with her husband, Mike, and her husky, Radar.

Index